Buddhism and Christianity

JOE WALKER & PATRICIA WATSON

Series Editor: Robert McVeigh

Hodder Gibson

A MEMBER OF THE HODDER HEADLINE GROUP

The Publishers would like to thank the following for permission to reproduce copyright material:
Photo credits p.4 © Alison Wright/CORBIS; p.5 © John Birdsall Photography; p.6 left top Phanie Agency / Rex Features, right top Lynsey Addario/ Corbis, for The New York Times, bottom © Reuters/Jose Manuel Ribeiro /CORBIS; p.7 left top © Kevin Fleming/CORBIS, right top Doug Steley / Alamy, bottom Janine Wiedel Photolibrary / Alamy; p.20 (all) James Osmond / Alamy; p.23 PHOTOTAKE Inc / Alamy; p.24 © BRECELJ BOJAN/CORBIS SYGMA; p.33 left Niall McDiarmid / Alamy, right top ArkReligion.com / Alamy, second top © Alison Wright/CORBIS, middle Maciej Wojtkowiak / Alamy, second bottom Mediacolor's / Alamy, bottom Simon Taplin /Asia Images / Getty Images; p.43 left ©2003 Charles Walker / Topfoto, right South West Images Scotland / Alamy; p.45 Jim Batty / Alamy; p.46 Ani Chudrun; p.47 Colin McPherson/Scottish Viewpoint; p.49 David Levenson / Alamy; p.51 courtesy of ROKPA INTERNATIONAL; p.55 © Werner Forman/CORBIS; p.57 top left © Ric Ergenbright/CORBIS, centre © Jeremy Horner/CORBIS, right © Tiziana and Gianni Baldizzone/CORBIS, bottom Eddie Gerald / Alamy; p.58 © Tibor Bognár/CORBIS; p.67 Mark Boulton / Alamy; p.68 Salvation Army; p.71 akg-images / Pietro Baguzzi; p.72 Network Photographers / Alamy; p.73 World Religions Photo Library / Alamy; p.74 V&A Images / Alamy; p.75 Bildarchiv Monheim GmbH / Alamy; p.76 © Bettmann/CORBIS; p.81 David Robertson / Alamy; p.86 Christian Ecology Link (CEL); p.93 Westend61 / Alamy; p.94 top © Bogdan Cristel/Reuters/Corbis, middle Andre Jenny / Alamy, bottom Westend61 / Alamy; p.97 Network Photographers / Alamy; p.102 © Ramin Talaie/Corbis; p.105 Visual&Written SL / Alamy.
Acknowledgements p.44–45 © The Telegraph, 1997; p.65–66 © Christian Aid. Used with permission. p.86 Text from Christian Ecology Link website reproduced with permission of CEL.
Artwork by Mary Hall and Clive Spong (Linden Artists).
Every effort has been made to trace all copyright holders, but if any have been inadvertently overlooked the Publishers will be pleased to make the necessary arrangements at the first opportunity.

Although every effort has been made to ensure that website addresses are correct at time of going to press, Hodder Gibson cannot be held responsible for the content of any website mentioned in this book. It is sometimes possible to find a relocated web page by typing in the address of the home page for a website in the URL window of your browser.

Orders: please contact Bookpoint Ltd, 130 Milton Park, Abingdon, Oxon OX14 4SB. Telephone: (44) 01235 827720. Fax: (44) 01235 400454. Lines are open from 9.00–5.00, Monday to Saturday, with a 24-hour message answering service. Visit our website at www.hoddereducation.co.uk. Hodder Gibson can be contacted direct on: Tel: 0141 848 1609; Fax: 0141 889 6315; email: hoddergibson@hodder.co.uk

© Joe Walker, Patricia Watson 2006
First published in 2006 by
Hodder Gibson, a member of the Hodder Headline Group
2a Christie Street
Paisley PA1 1NB

Impression number   10 9 8 7 6 5 4 3 2 1
Year   2010 2009 2008 2007 2006

Cover photo Top row: left and right, Corel Corporation; second left, PhotoDisc. Second row: left, PhotoDisc; centre and right, Corel Corporation. Third row: left, Corel Corporation; right, Digital Vision/Getty Images. Bottom row: left, PhotoDisc Green/Getty Images; right, Corel Corporation.
Typeset in 12 on 14pt Giovanni by
Phoenix Photosetting, Chatham, Kent
Printed and bound in Italy

A catalogue record for this title is available from the British Library

ISBN-10: 0 340-88990-X
ISBN-13: 978-0-340-88990-9

Contents

Teacher's Notes

Personal Search

This series of books is aimed at P7–S2 pupils. The authors believe that 'personal search' lies at the heart of religious and moral education (RME) and is 'a process by which pupils can discover and develop their own beliefs and values.' *(Effective Teaching of Religious and Moral Education: Personal Search*, LT Scotland 2001) This definition is in keeping with the National Guidelines: Religious and Moral Education 5–14 which states that one of the aims of RME is for pupils to 'to develop their own beliefs, attitudes, moral values and practices through a process of personal search, discovery and critical evaluation.'

The study of religions

The authors believe that RME is essentially about the study of religions and this study has a significant role to play in personal search in developing pupils' beliefs and values. Although a pupil's beliefs and values develop in a number of ways both within and outside school, the study of religions provides a distinctive approach.

It is helpful to study religion through its central features. The National Guidelines identify five key features – celebrations, festivals, ceremonies and customs; sacred writings, stories and key figures; beliefs; sacred places, worship and symbols (practices); moral values and attitudes. In these Personal Search books each religion is explored through units relating to each of the key features as set out below.

Each book covers two religions. Religions have been paired according to their dates of origins: Hinduism and Judaism are the earliest, then Buddhism and Christianity, and finally Islam and Sikhism.

Although there is no explicit study of non-religious systems of belief such as Humanism, there are opportunities to consider non-religious stances for living, as well as religious stances, on issues such as the

	Festivals and celebrations	Stories and key figures	Beliefs	Practices	Values
Buddhism	Ordination	The Buddha's teaching	Impermanence	Meditation	Karuna
Christianity	Easter	The Sermon on the Mount	Creation	Holy Communion	Agape
Hinduism	Samskaras	The Ramayana	Reincarnation	Puja	Dharma
Judaism	Yom Kippur	The story of Esther	Suffering	Kashrut	Tzedakah
Islam	Ramadan	Muhammad	Submission	Hajj	Ummah
Sikhism	The Khalsa	Guru Granth Sahib	Mool Mantra	The Langar	Vand Chhakna

origins of the universe, the existence of God, suffering and evil, relationships and moral values.

Stimulus material

Each unit contains stimulus material for pupils to engage with. This includes texts, stories, creedal statements, personal testimonies and experiences. The aim of the stimulus material is to involve pupils in dialogue with religions so that they can find out about the beliefs and values of religious believers in an atmosphere of enquiry, openness and critical discussion.

Teaching and learning

Each unit begins with a statement of the content to be covered and identifies the main concepts and themes. Personal search questions and activities focus on these concepts and themes. The units make use of a process to enhance personal search which was first introduced in *Effective Teaching of Religious and Moral Education: Personal Search* (LT Scotland 2001). This process has **three** stages:

- Finding out
- Making connections
- Thinking it over

Finding out
This involves finding out about the beliefs, values and practices of religious traditions. Pupils should be encouraged to appreciate the importance of knowledge and evidence as the basis for developing their own beliefs and values, and for justifying their own opinions.

Making connections
This involves connecting other people's beliefs, values and practices to pupils' own ideas and life experiences. Pupils' experiences of family, friendships and belonging to a community already shape their intellectual, social and moral development. This stage provides opportunities for pupils to reflect, talk about and share their own ideas and experiences.

Thinking it over
This involves creating opportunities for dialogue around the concepts and themes that emerge from the study of religions and pupils' own experience of life. Thinking it over should be challenging, dealing with issues that push children's thinking beyond the immediate knowledge of the content. The issues will invite discussion on a range of questions to do with God, suffering, evil, right and wrong, life and death, relationships, moral and social values, and the nature and origins of the natural world.

The three stages of the process need not take place in the order in which they are set out above. A unit may begin by finding out more about a religion, or perhaps by connecting with some aspect of pupil experience, or even by raising an issue for discussion. It is likely that discussion and activities will move backwards and forwards between each stage of the process.

Activities
Within the 'finding out' activities there are opportunities for further investigation and research. Pupils will need access to other resources including books, audio-visual materials and the Internet. In some of the 'making connections' and 'thinking it over' questions and activities teachers might encourage pupils to work together in small groups to discuss, share ideas and exchange views.

Choosing religions and units

There is no prescribed order in which religions or units within a religion should be studied. Schools might study one or more religions or select units from across religions using the key features.

Progression

The three books in this series provide materials for pupils throughout P7–S2. Pupils' maturity of thinking will develop over the three years, as will their reading, writing and interpretation skills. The units vary in terms of language level and difficulty of questions and tasks. Consequently, teachers should be selective with regard to these depending on pupils' age, stage and abilities. Attainment targets from the National Guidelines have not been included but teachers should use the Guidelines to ensure that pupils achieve their full potential.

Assessment

By looking at pupil responses to the various tasks, talking to individual pupils about their responses, and listening to pupils' discussion, teachers will be able to gather evidence about pupils' personal search skills. Pupils, through completing the activities in the books, should be able to state their views clearly on issues associated with the concepts identified at the beginning of each unit. They should be able to support these views with reasons and evidence in writing or in speech, and at some length. If pupils do this, they are demonstrating personal search skills.

Buddhism

The Buddha's Teaching

The religion of Buddhism is based on the teachings of Gotama Buddha who lived in the country now known as Nepal, during the sixth century BCE. The Buddha began his life as Prince Siddhatta but as a young man he decided to leave behind his life of wealth and privilege. He studied and meditated and eventually found enlightenment and the answers to some important questions about life.

IN THIS SECTION YOU WILL BE ASKED TO THINK ABOUT ...

✓ Selfishness and greed
✓ Suffering
✓ Right and wrong actions
✓ Wisdom
✓ Dissatisfaction

stimulus 1

Accounts of the Buddha's life

Here are stories from three people who knew the Buddha at different stages in his life.

Hello, my name is **Asita**. I was well known in the Kingdom of Kapilavatthu where the Buddha was born. Soon after his birth I was called to the palace by his father King Suddhodana and asked to predict the young prince's future. Even at that early stage, it wasn't hard to tell that he would eventually become a Buddha – an Enlightened One. I could see the mark of wisdom in him. He was without question destined for future greatness. I wasn't surprised to hear that he started meditating at a very early age.

I am **King Suddhodana**, head of the Sakya clan and ruler of the Kingdom of Kapilavatthu. It's hard for me to admit it but I was devastated by Asita's predictions for my son Siddhatta. I had hoped that one day he would inherit my Kingdom and continue the traditions of our great family. His mother Queen Maya had died soon after his birth in Lumbini; I could not stand the thought of losing him also. I vowed to keep him protected within the walls of the palace. If he never saw the outside world then perhaps he would not want to go there. I gave him everything a young boy could want to make him happy.

Hi! My name's **Channa**. I worked in the palace and became a loyal servant to the young prince Siddhatta. For years the King kept his son confined to the area within the palace walls. Everything he wanted was provided for him – he even had a palace for every season of the year! But he wasn't allowed to go out.

He was a curious lad though, desperate to find out more about the world he lived in. I was nervous the day he asked me to take him outside, but how could I refuse? He was my master. All I could do was try my best to ensure his safety outside the palace.

❶ Start a fact-file about the Buddha using the information in Stimulus 1. Include the following information:
- His original name.
- His parents.
- Place of birth.
- Family background.
- Upbringing.
- Personality.

❷ Kapilavatthu no longer exists but Lumbini does. It's in the country of Nepal just north of the border with India. Get an atlas and find out where this is. Trace a map of India and Nepal and mark Lumbini on it.

❸ Why was Asita called to the palace?

❹ Why was King Suddhodana so upset by Asita's predictions? What did he decide to do?

❺ Suggest two reasons why Siddhatta wanted to see beyond the palace. Why do you think Channa was nervous about taking the Prince out of the palace?

❻ Explain what you think it means to become 'enlightened'.

The garden where Buddha was born in Lumbini in Nepal

MAKING CONNECTIONS

❶ If Siddhatta had been born nowadays, what sort of life would he have as a royal prince? Use pictures from magazines and catalogues to create a collage entitled 'A Life of Luxury'. You could do this as a whole class.

❷ There's a saying 'money can't buy happiness'. Do you believe this? Give reasons for your answer.

❸ Imagine you had been kept in your bedroom since birth. What would you need to make you happy? How could you learn things about the world outside your room? How would you feel? What would you miss out on? Write a poem or song entitled 'Trapped in My Room'.

❹ How much do your parents influence your decisions in life? When you leave school, will you do what they want you to do or do you have other ideas? Do you ever argue with them about your future?

❺ Even today some people claim they can predict the future. What are these people called? Why is astrology still important? How does it influence people's lives nowadays?

❻ Which sign of the zodiac were you born under? Do you read your horoscope? Why/why not? Do you think our lives are influenced by the stars in any way?

Thinking it over

❶ Asita says he saw the mark of wisdom in the young child. What does wisdom mean? How can you tell if someone is wise or not? In a group try to make a list of people you know about who might be considered as wise.

❷ Work with a partner. Each of you should choose one of the following views to present in a paired discussion. You should prepare for the discussion by trying to think of arguments to support your chosen point of view.

> The King showed wisdom by keeping his son in the palace.

> The King was not wise to keep his son confined to the palace.

❸ Do you think someone can be wise if very young? How might someone become wise? Can anyone become wise or do you have to be someone special?

stimulus

2 *The Four Sights*

On their trip outside of the palace, Prince Siddhatta saw many things for the first time. He was constantly asking Channa questions… but there were four sights which really made him stop and think. These things are still common in our world!

> Channa, why do these people have skin which is wrinkled and bodies which look worn out? How can they cope with life?

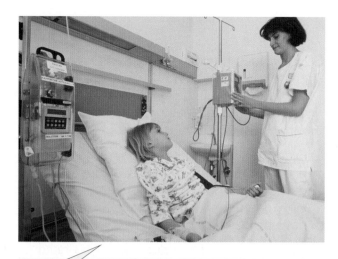

Channa, why is this child needing such care? Why can't she get up and play with friends? What will become of her?

Channa, what is happening here? Everyone looks so sad! Why do they put the bodies of loved ones in the ground?

Channa, why have these people chosen a different way of life? They look so peaceful. What is the truth they hold?

❶ Add details of this episode to your fact-file about the Buddha.

❷ Draw a circle divided into four segments. Think of a symbol to represent each of the Four Sights and draw them into the segments of your circle. Make sure your symbols will help you remember what the Four Sights are.

❸ Write a script for the conversation between Siddhatta and Channa during the journey. Use the questions in Stimulus 2 to help you, but make up the answers you think Channa might have given the young prince.

❹ Why do you think these sights made Siddhatta think so much?

MAKING CONNECTIONS

❶ Many people from this country have gone to live in poorer places in order to help those worse off. Find out about the work of an individual who has dedicated their life to helping others and write a report about the work they do. Try to explain why they chose to give up their life of comfort.

❷ Collect pictures of people suffering and working hard to earn a living. Create a collage of these pictures and display it opposite your Life of Luxury collage. Discuss the contrast between the two sets of images. Is it fair that life is so difficult for many people in our world?

❸ How might rich people help those less fortunate? Try to make a list of at least five things they could do. Do you think we all have a responsibility to help those who are suffering? Why/why not?

Thinking it over

❶ Here are three pictures.

  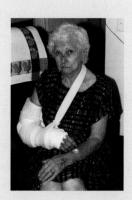

Which picture makes you feel most sad? Why? What could you do to help the person you have chosen? Is it easy or difficult to ignore the amount of suffering in our world?

❷ Why do old age, sickness and death often make us unhappy? Can anything be done to make these times less difficult for people? Copy and complete the following table to keep a note of your ideas about this:

	It's a difficult time because...	It could be easier if people...
Growing old		
Getting sick		
Dying		

❸ Siddhatta thought that the holy men he saw were more peaceful looking than all the other people. Do you think religion can bring peace into people's lives? How do you think a religious faith might help those who are suffering in the world? Interview a religious person about this if you can.

stimulus
3

Prince Siddhatta becomes the Buddha

The Kingdom of Kapilavatthu is in shock this morning as we finally gain confirmation that Prince Siddhatta has indeed left home for good. It seems that he has cast aside all his money and power and has suggested that his son Rahula become heir to the throne. Rumours have been circulating since the Prince's chariot was seen visiting various parts of the Kingdom a few months ago.

Our reporter has at last managed to secure an exclusive interview with Channa, the Prince's closest servant. Here is his story:

'After that trip out of the palace, Prince Siddhatta was never the same again. He couldn't settle back into palace routine and was forever asking questions about the lives of ordinary people in the Kingdom. I knew it would only be a matter of time before he wanted to go out again, but what a shock I got when it happened! As we approached the edge of the forest, he ordered me to stop the chariot so he could get down. After a few moments of quiet meditation, he removed all his fine clothes and wrapped himself in a simple yellow cloth. He told me to sell his clothes and give the money to the poor. He said he needed to search for the truth about suffering because he wanted to help his people. I was speechless – before I could say a word he took out his sword and cut off all his beautiful hair! I almost wept with grief. Surely my master had gone mad! It seems not though. He told me to go back to the palace but I followed him and have kept close watch on him this past few months – I didn't want any harm to come to him. What he has done has been truly amazing. First I saw him practise all forms of mental discipline and deep meditation with the highest gurus in the land. Then I watched in fear as he appeared to be pushing his body to every extreme, only eating a few grains of rice a day and becoming so thin he could touch his spine from the stomach. I feared he might die until one day he suddenly seemed to gain control of himself again. He sat down under a Bodhi Tree in Bodhgaya and remained there meditating until he found Enlightenment. To see him now is awesome. He has an aura about him which is indescribable. People come from all over to hear his words. He has truly fulfilled Asita's prophecy.'

❶ Add the details of this story to your fact-file on the Buddha.

❷ How do you think King Suddhodana would feel about his son's decision? Write his story for *The Sakya Star* newspaper.

❸ Describe the two types of self-discipline the Prince tried out. What do you think he was hoping to achieve through these practices? Why didn't he continue with them?

❹ Write a postcard from Siddhatta to his father. Try to explain what he meant by 'searching for the truth about suffering'.

❺ Use an atlas to find out where Bodhgaya is and mark it on your map.

❻ Design a travel page about Bodhgaya. Find some pictures on the Internet and explain why this is a major place of pilgrimage for Buddhists. Here are a few useful sites to get you started:

- www.pilgrimage-india.com
- www.sacredsites.com
- www.indiatravelog.com
- www.buddhanet.net
- www.cultural-heritage-india.com

❼ Which of these two words would you choose to describe Prince Siddhatta:

Selfish   **Selfless**

Give a reason for your choice.

❽ Do you think Prince Siddhatta would have been happy if he had stayed in the palace and become the next King? Give reasons for your answer.

MAKING CONNECTIONS

❶ Here's a letter recently sent to a problem page. In what ways is Joe suffering? In what ways are his parents suffering? Write a reply to Joe from the Buddha.

❷ What does it mean to practise self-discipline? How much self-discipline do you think you have? How can having self-discipline help you to achieve your goals in life? Is it easy to have self-discipline? Why/why not?

❸ The Prince gave up everything in order to find the Truth he was seeking. What goals do you have in your life? What would you be prepared to give up in order to achieve your goals?

❹ Buddhists travel from all over the world to Bodhgaya. Write about a place that is special to you. It could be a place you have been to or a place you'd really like to see. Why is that place so important to you?

Dear Marge,

In a few months I will be leaving school ready to start university. I would like to take a year out first and travel a bit. I'm desperate to see more of the world first hand. I'm fed up with studying right now and want to learn more practical skills. However, my parents think that it's just a skive I'm after. They say that if I don't go straight to university they won't continue to support me financially. They want me to get a good job as soon as possible and a good house like theirs. I love them very much and don't want to upset them.

What should I do?

Yours truly

Joe

Thinking it over

❶ Siddhatta wanted to know the answer to the question 'Why do people suffer?' Are there any 'big questions' about the world which you'd like answered? Brainstorm in your class and make a display of these questions. Why do so many of our questions seem impossible to answer?

❷ 'Those who suffer most are those who deserve it most.' Do you agree or disagree? Give reasons for your answer.

stimulus 4

The Buddha's first sermon

After his Enlightenment, the Buddha gave his first teachings to a group of monks at the Deer Park in **Benares**. He was thought to be about 35 years old. He felt that he had found the truth about suffering which he had been searching for and now needed to pass that message on to others. This is what made him a **Fully Enlightened Buddha** – not only did he understand suffering but he was also able to help others understand it. In this sermon he taught the **Four Noble Truths**:

* Life is full of dissatisfaction (**Dukkha**).
* Our dissatisfaction is caused by our own selfish desires and greed (**Tanha**).
* It is possible to stop these feelings of greed and selfishness (**Nirodha**).
* The way to stop them is the Eightfold Path (**Magga**).

The Eightfold Path is a code of guidance for a Buddhist life. Buddhists believe that following this path will eventually lead to enlightenment. Going through life without this kind of support is like crossing a river without stepping stones. It's sometimes called the **Middle Way** as it aims to help Buddhists avoid the one extreme of total indulgence in luxurious pleasures and the other extreme of complete self-denial.

The Eightfold Path

Right View
Right Intention
Right Speech
Right Action
Right Livelihood
Right Effort
Right Mindfulness
Right Concentration

❶ Benares is just outside the Indian city of Varanasi on the banks of the River Ganges. Find this in an atlas and mark it on your map.

❷ Working as a group, discuss the meaning of the Buddha's sermon. Create a storyboard with lots of pictures to illustrate the Four Noble Truths.

❸ Stimulus 4 shows the Eightfold Path as a set of stepping stones. Buddhists often explain it as a wheel with eight spokes. Think of another good symbol for the path. Make a poster for your classroom wall.

❹ What is meant by Dukkha? How had the Buddha experienced Dukkha in his life?

❺ How did the Buddha try to overcome Tanha in his own life?

❻ What do you think is meant by 'luxurious pleasures' and 'complete self denial'?

❼ What does the word 'indulgence' mean? Is indulgence good or bad?

❽ Explain what is meant by 'going through life without this kind of support is like crossing a river without stepping stones'.

❾ Why is the Eightfold Path often called the Middle Way?

MAKING CONNECTIONS

❶ Think about your week so far. How much Dukkha have you experienced?
   a) Make a list of all the times you have felt annoyed, bored, confused, angry, sad or any other type of dissatisfaction.
   b) Now look back over your list. How many of these things were your own fault? Choose one thing that has happened and write about how you could have avoided Dukkha by acting differently.

❷ The Eightfold Path is a set of principles by which to live. What are your principles in life? Draw your own stepping stones with your principles engraved on them. Why is it useful to have a set of principles to guide your actions in life? What if you didn't have them?

stimulus 5 *Living the Eightfold Path*

Get some counters and a dice. Play the game of snakes and ladders to find out more about the steps of the Eightfold Path.

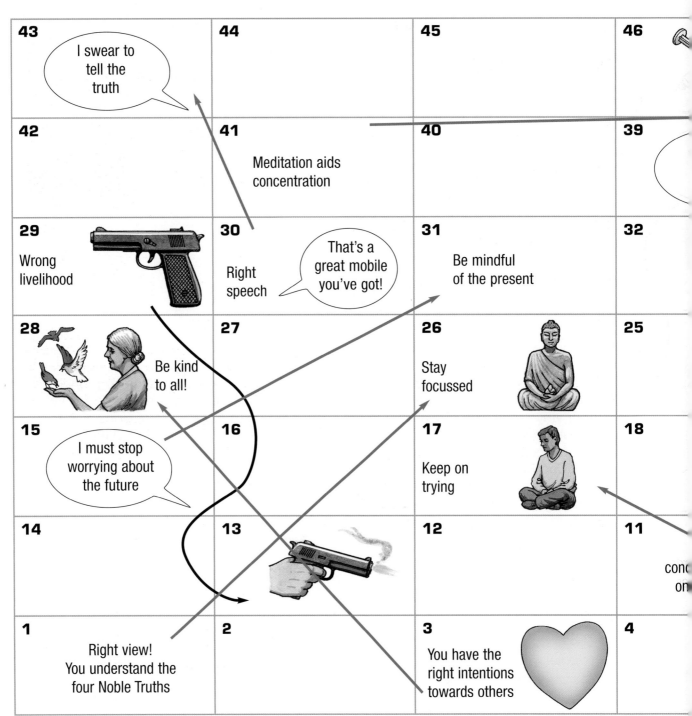

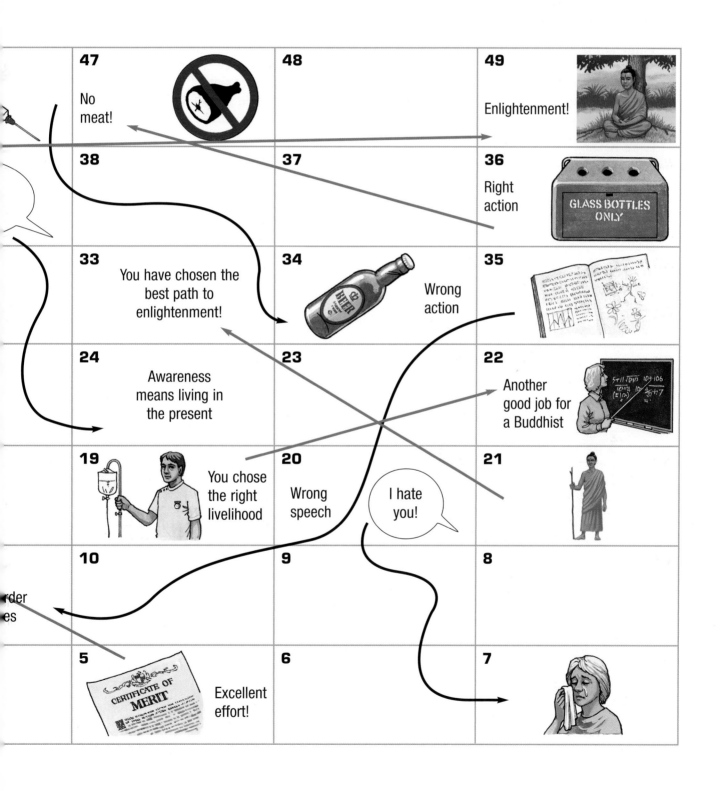

❶ Copy and complete this table using the information from the Snakes & Ladders game to help you. See if you can add some ideas of your own too!

Eightfold Path	This means:
Right view	
Right intention	
Right speech	
Right action	
Right livelihood	
Right effort	
Right mindfulness	
Right concentration	

❷ How is the Eightfold Path similar to the Precepts which Buddhist monks must follow?

❸ The illustration below shows some other examples of things the Buddha taught. Try to explain each of the sayings in your own words. Which part of the Eightfold Path does each one relate to?

Overcome anger by love; overcome wrong by good; overcome the miserly by generosity, and the liar by truth.

Why do I, being subject to birth, decay, disease, death, sorrow and impurities, thus search after things of like nature. How do I, who am subject to things of such nature, realise their disadvantages and seek after the unattained, unsurpassed, perfect security which is Nibbana!

Easy to do are things that are bad and not beneficial to self; But very, very hard to do indeed is that which is beneficial and good.

Whoever does wrong to an innocent person, or to one who is pure and harmless, the wrong returns to that fool just like fine dust thrown against the wind.

Support for one's parents, assistance to one's wife and children, consistency in one's work. This is the highest protection.

MAKING CONNECTIONS

❶ Look though some recent newspapers and cut out stories about bad things which have happened. Work as a group to discuss which parts of the Eightfold Path each story relates to. Explain how following the Eightfold Path would help to make the world a better place.

❷ a) Which part of the Eightfold Path would you find most difficult? Why?

b) Which part of the Eightfold Path would you find easiest? Why?

❸ Do you eat meat? Do you have a pet? Have you ever been to the circus or visited a zoo? Discuss the different ways animals are treated in our society. What do you think is right or wrong?

❹ Think of a time when you argued with someone. Whose fault was the argument? Did you say things you wish you hadn't? Could you have avoided the argument by thinking more carefully about what you said? How easy is it to control our speech?

❺ Do you agree with the Buddha's teachings about not using violence? Is the use of violence ever acceptable?

❻ Are you ever lazy? Do you do enough to help at home? Could you sometimes work harder at school? Have you ever missed out on things because you 'just couldn't be bothered'? How does laziness sometimes affect the quality of our lives?

❼ Write a short story entitled 'It was certainly worth the effort!' Your story should be about a time when you didn't want to do something at first but it turned out well.

Thinking it over

❶ Is the world really as bad as the Buddha seems to suggest?

❷ What does it mean to be selfish? Why do you think people are selfish? Is it possible to stop being selfish? Have you ever been selfish?

❸ What does it mean to be greedy? What kinds of things are people greedy for? Make a list of the things people feel greedy about and arrange them in order of importance.

❹ How easy is it to change your behaviour and adopt new habits?

❺ Does being satisfied with life depend on what choices we make? What kinds of choices might lead to satisfaction or dissatisfaction?

❻ Following the Eightfold Path is a real challenge for Buddhists. Is the Buddha asking too much?

❼ Do you think the Prince discovered the Truth about why there is so much suffering in the world?

Impermanence

The Buddha taught that impermanence is a fact of life. It is one of the three marks of human existence. He saw that much of the suffering which people experience in life is because they cannot accept that everything changes. He tried to get people to realise the importance of this aspect of life and encouraged people to be more able to let go of things which cannot last.

stimulus 1

Experiences of Impermanence

IN THIS SECTION YOU WILL BE ASKED TO THINK ABOUT ...

✓ The way everything around us is constantly changing.

✓ The need to accept changes within our personal lives.

✓ Letting go of things which can't last.

✓ Coping with loss.

✓ Death and afterlife.

I feel really sad today. Last night Mum took our pet labrador Sadie to the vets to be put to sleep. Sadie had been ill for a long time and was getting on a bit but I kept hoping she'd recover. For the past week and a half she's not done much but sleep. The vet had given us some medicine to help her feel more comfortable but it was obvious she wasn't going to get any better. It feels really strange in the house today. She's been around as long as I can remember and we've had such a lot of fun together. I am really going to miss her.

Rasmia

I'm going to kill my wee brother when I get my hands on him! He's only gone and broken my Game Boy hasn't he? I keep telling him not to go into my room but he never listens. I saved up my pocket money for months to buy that and then put all my birthday money in the pot too. I'll never be able to replace it.

Susan

Today we went to visit my gran in the nursing home. She has Alzheimer's Disease and that means she can hardly recognise any of us anymore. It must be horrible for Dad to see his Mum like that but he still goes to see her every day. Last night I heard him telling my Mum that he doesn't think she'll be around for next Christmas. I feel so helpless, there's nothing I can do but I don't want Gran to die!

David

I hate getting out of bed in the wintertime. It's so cold and dark outside and the days seem so short. You drive to work in the dark and you drive home in the dark. It makes me feel really miserable. I long for the spring to come and for the lighter evenings so that the kids can play outside more and I can spend time in the garden and go for walks in the evening. It's nice when it snows but even that doesn't happen very often anymore!

John

FINDING OUT

❶ Read each of the stories in Stimulus 1. What do the four people have in common with each other?

❷ Copy and complete this table to list the feelings each person is probably experiencing at this time in their life.

	What's happening in their lives?	How is this making them feel?
Rasmia		
Susan		
David		
John		

❸ What does the word impermanence mean? Make a list of things which are impermanent.

❹ The Buddha talked a lot about impermanence. He said that people should always remember 'nothing lasts forever'. How might this teaching help Rasmia, Susan, David and John through their difficult situations?

❺ Choose one of the characters from Stimulus 1. Write a letter from the Buddha explaining the importance of recognising that 'nothing lasts forever'. Try to write something that will help the person through their difficult time.

MAKING CONNECTIONS

❶ Think about how much your emotions change, even in the course of just one day. Draw a diagram to show your highs and lows throughout a typical day.

❷ Choose one of the emotions from the list below. Write about a time when you have felt this emotion quite strongly. Describe what happened and how you managed to cope.

Sadness   Anger   Misery
Worry   Frustration

❸ Think about how your life has changed since you were a baby. Are there people or things which used to be really important to you that aren't so important now? How has your appearance changed?

stimulus
2 Interview with a Buddhist monk

Class 1B went on a visit to a Buddhist monastery. Mrs Wright had given them all a topic to find out more about. Steve and Rajiv had been given the topic Impermanence and were instructed to interview Karma Lonsang to find out more about the Buddha's teachings on this. Here is an extract from their interview:

Steve: Is there a Buddhist word for impermanence?

Karma Lonsang: Oh yes, the Buddha used the word Anicca. This word brings together the idea of everything constantly changing and the fact that nothing lasts forever.

Rajiv: Both of these things seem quite obvious to me most of the time – why did the Buddha make such a fuss about impermanence?

Karma Lonsang: You're right! Impermanence is pretty obvious, so obvious in fact that the Buddha spoke about it as a truth – a basic fact of life. Not something we should fuss about but instead something we should learn to accept. Experience of impermanence in our lives is unavoidable. It's something we all have to come to terms with.

Steve: So like Rajiv said, what's the big fuss?

Karma Lonsang: Well the problem is that for lots of people it's difficult to accept impermanence even though it's in every aspect of our lives. We are constantly reminded of the Buddha's teaching in everything around us but people don't like to think about it. Most folk hate it when there are big changes in their lives and for many people, coping with the loss of a loved one is almost impossible to bear. It's natural to want the good things in our lives to last forever.

Rajiv: I know what you mean. When my Granddad died last year I thought my Mum would never be happy again. She still finds it difficult to smile some days. I really miss him too.

Karma Lonsang: Yes it's hard to lose someone you love, but Anicca applies to so many things. Everything about us is impermanent. We all know it's natural to grow old and wrinkled but look how much money is spent on creams, lotions and treatments by people trying to stay looking young.

Steve: And we all know in our heads that things will get broken and it's not really the end of the world when that happens, but it can feel like it at the time!

Karma Lonsang: You're right again Steve and that's the biggest problem about impermanence. When we are happy and content with everything in our world we forget that change is a natural, normal part of life and so when change happens we are so surprised, we often react badly.

Rajiv: Or even overreact, like when you discovered that your favourite DVD was all scratched and wouldn't play anymore. Remember that Steve?

Steve: Yes I do – I thought it was your fault and didn't speak to you for days. We almost stopped being friends over it!

Karma Lonsang: Now that would've been a shame! You see, the Buddha taught that we need to keep things in perspective in our lives. Even when we are sad or feel angry or some other bad thing, we should remember that the bad times won't last forever either. We need to remember that all change is natural.

Rajiv: Then things wouldn't come as such a shock to us and we'd be able to cope better with everything life throws at us.

Karma Lonsang: We'd even be able to get through little ups and downs more easily – like when we are bored during a lesson at school, or a bit fed-up because we have no one to play with. When you feel these kinds of things just keep remembering Anicca – nothing lasts forever!

Steve: But surely that means the good times won't last either!

Karma Lonsang: You're dead right – so don't ever take them for granted.

FINDING OUT

❶ Work with a couple of other people to read over the interview extract in Stimulus 2. Discuss what you think Karma Lonsang is saying about impermanence.

❷ What is the Buddhist word for impermanence? What two ideas does this word bring together?

❸ The Buddha taught that impermanence is a 'fact of life'. What does this mean? Do you think he is right?

❹ How did the Buddha come to realise that nothing lasts forever? What examples of impermanence did he encounter in his own life? (Look back at the chapter on the life of the Buddha.)

❺ What advice do you think the Buddha would give to people who are unhappy about some things in life?

❻ Choose **one** of the following situations and try to explain how the Buddha's teaching on impermanence might help:

If your house was destroyed by fire.	If you failed an exam which would help you get into university.	If your best friend emigrated to Australia.

MAKING CONNECTIONS

❶ Have you ever noticed how much you might change even in the space of a few hours? Keep a diary for a week. Write about how your moods change throughout each day. What things happen to put you in a bad mood or a good mood? What makes you bored? Excited? Worried? How quickly do your moods change? Write it all down!

❷ Some changes are easier to see happening than others. Can you list some changes we see and others we don't see so easily?

Thinking it over

❶ Work with a partner. Imagine that you are Steve and Rajiv arguing over the scratched DVD. First act out the scene so that it has an unhappy ending with the two of you falling out. Then try it again and think of a way to resolve the argument so that you stay friends. Try to include something about the Buddha's teaching in your story.

❷ Do you think the Buddha is correct when he says 'nothing lasts forever'? Can you think of anything which does last?

❸ What kind of changes in life are easy to accept and which are more difficult?

❹ 'We can't control the changes in our lives, but we can control how we react to them.' Do you think this is true? What difference do our reactions to situations make? Can you think of some situations when it might be useful to control your reactions?

3 Impermanence in nature

MAKING CONNECTIONS

❶ Look at the pictures in Stimulus 3. Explain how the tree continually changes throughout the year.

❷ What other things in nature are also constantly changing?

❸ In what ways does nature help to remind us of the Buddha's teaching about Anicca?

❹ Choose your own examples of impermanence in nature and draw some pictures to illustrate how things keep changing in the world around us. If you prefer you could collect pictures from magazines and make a collage for your classroom wall.

4 *The Buddha teaches about Impermanence*

King Pasendikosala was very sad because his wife had died.

When he heard that the Buddha was collecting alms near the palace, he sent his servant to invite the Buddha to have breakfast with him.

When the Buddha arrived at the palace he said he didn't want any breakfast. Instead he wanted to go for a walk and have a look at the royal garage. The king said they could do this as long as the Buddha stayed for breakfast afterwards.

After breakfast the Buddha taught the King about how the human body decays.

'Think of how your royal carts used to look' he said. 'They were once beautifully decorated and regularly used, but now they are old and need many repairs. They cannot fulfil their function because they are so old. In fact the beautiful carts you once had are really no longer there. They were just temporary. A set of items put together for a set purpose with a limited existence.'

'This is just like us. Our bodies are temporary – put together for a short time but like all things they must come to an end.'

The Buddha taught that as humans we are made up of **Five Skandhas** or 'bundles of things':

- **A physical body** – how we look.
- **Senses** – what we experience in relation to the world around us.
- **Thoughts** – the connection between our senses and our mind.
- **Awareness** – knowing that we are alive and being conscious of the world around us.
- **Ideas** – how we decide what to do at any point in time.

When we die these things no longer exist in the same way. Buddhists use the word Anatta to describe this belief that there is nothing of the human being which exists beyond the death. According to the Buddha, there is nothing permanent about human beings.

FINDING OUT

❶ Explain how the Buddha helped King Pasendikosala come to terms with the death of his wife.

❷ In what way did the Buddha suggest we are just like the carts?

❸ On another occasion the Buddha was called in to help a queen who was so beautiful she could not bear to think of ever growing old and losing her beauty. Draw your own story board and complete the story to show how the Buddha might make her realise that everyone grows old and gets wrinkled.

❹ What are the Five Skandhas? How are they connected to each other?

❺ What does the word Anatta mean?

❻ Draw a self-portrait or stick a photo of yourself in your jotter. Label the picture with the Five Skandhas.

MAKING CONNECTIONS

❶ Ask everyone in your class to bring in a photo of themselves as a baby. Hold a competition to see if you can guess who's who. Choose three of the photos and compare them to the people you now know. What things are the same about each person and what things are different?

❷ What things do you think will change over the next ten years? Try to draw a caricature of how your best friend might look in ten years' time. If you lost touch and met up again after a few years how might you know it was the same person?

❸ When someone close to us dies it is often very difficult for us to accept this change. Why do you think this is? What kind of things do people often say to comfort those who are grieving? How might the Buddha's teaching help us to accept death as a natural part of life?

Thinking it over

❶ The Buddha says there is nothing of the human being which exists beyond death. Do you think the Buddha's view of a human being is correct? Is there anything else you can think of which is an essential part of being human? Do you think any part of us lives on after death? Give reasons for your answer.

❷ Some other religions teach that we all have a permanent soul which continues to exist after death. What do you think about this belief? Do you think there is any reason to believe in the existence of a soul? If so, what might be its purpose? How might believing in a soul help people to cope when a loved one dies?

Buddhist Mandalas – the art of impermanence

Dear Hannah

As you know I have recently been on holiday to America. We had a great time – saw all the famous sights you would imagine and completely stuffed ourselves on the biggest hamburgers ever. You wouldn't believe the amount of stuff we brought home, everything is sooo cheap! Last week I got my photos back and suddenly I was reminded about something we saw at a museum in Boston. Knowing how interested you are in Buddhism, I thought you'd like to know about this. In the middle of the foyer there were a couple of Buddhist monks sitting surrounded by bags and bags of coloured sand, creating a huge pattern on the floor. They both had a little brass funnel about ten inches long in each hand. The opening at the bottom of each funnel was so small it could only let a few grains of sand through at a time. The outline of the pattern was drawn with chalk and so they worked together very carefully to cover the design with the coloured sand by gentling rubbing the two funnels together so that there was just enough encouragement for the sand inside to fall through onto the pattern. It was incredible to watch how much concentration they put into their work. Somehow they just managed to ignore all the tourists with constantly clicking cameras. We went there on the third day they had been working on it, so it was about two-thirds complete and looked really amazing. The museum guide told me that it was a special Tibetan type of art called a Mandala. This one in particular was called the Chenrezig Mandala. The monks were creating it in the hope of bringing peace and compassion into the world. The monks would work on it for about five days and then guess what?! I thought they would be putting a see-through cover over it so that it could be a permanent feature of the museum entrance but you'll never believe it – they swept it all up almost the minute it was complete! All that work for nothing. The sand was gathered up, put into a jar and poured into the Charles River. What a waste of all that time and effort eh? Just as well I took some pictures to send you. Hope you like them.

Write back soon and let me know how your trip to India was. Did you manage to meet the Dalai Lama?

Lots of love

Sarah

❶ What is a Mandala? Describe how a sand Mandala is made.

❷ Explain why the monks were creating the Chenrezig Mandala?

❸ Carry out some web research to find out more about the Chenrezig Mandala.

❹ Try to find pictures of other Buddhist Mandalas to display on your classroom wall. Try to find some information about the meaning within each pattern. www.himalayanart.org has information about several Mandala patterns. You could write poems to go with the display.

❺ How does creating a Mandala remind Buddhists of the teaching about impermanence?

❻ Sarah thinks that making the Mandala is a complete waste of time and effort. How would the Buddhist monks reply to her criticism?

❼ Before beginning the Mandala, Buddhist monks say prayers and even ask for the sand to be blessed. Why do you think they do this?

Stages of a Mandala

a) There is an opening ceremony to bless the site of the mandala and the materials being used.

b) The mandala is designed and the outline drawn.

c) Starting from the centre the brightly coloured sand is carefully placed in order to create the pattern.

d) When the mandala is completed, prayers are said to ask for blessings.

e) The mandala is destroyed. Starting from the outside edges the sand is brushed into the centre.

f) The sand is gathered into an urn and taken to be dispersed into flowing water while more prayers are said.

MAKING CONNECTIONS

❶ Design and create your own Mandala. Start by thinking about the things which are important in your life and choosing an image to symbolise each one. Use this planning table to help you:

What's important to me?	A symbol to represent this.	Colours I will use for these symbols.
People		
Places		
Objects		
Beliefs		

Create a basic shape for the background of your Mandala. Once you have your background you can start putting in the symbols. Try to make your pattern symmetrical. Take your time to colour it neatly and make the finished product something you are really proud of.

❷ Look carefully at your completed Mandala. How does it illustrate the impermanence within your life?

❸ Compare your Mandala with those of your friends in the class. What can you tell about each other from the Mandalas you've all drawn?

❹ How would you feel about destroying your Mandala?

stimulus
6 Learning about Impermanence

Here are some words of wisdom from a lay Buddhist who has often watched the Dalai Lama take a sweeping brush and destroy the Mandala which had taken a group of monks several days to create.

Destroying the Mandala is an important part of the ceremony. There is an impermanence, a transience in life that no one can stop. What we can control is how we choose to use this time – the only thing we have in our hands. Leading life in a purposeful, meaningful way does not necessarily mean having to be religious; it really means helping others and not being destructive to others. Those who wish to make their lives meaningful through religion can focus on incorporating the teachings of their beliefs into their actual daily acts.

Thinking it over

❶ What a waste of all that time and effort!

Destroying the Mandala is an important part of the ceremony.

Which of the two views do you agree with? Give reasons for your answer.

❷ What does the word 'transience' mean? How is this linked to the Mandala?

❸ 'What we can control is how we choose to use this time – the only thing we have in our hands.' Do you agree? Give reasons for your answer.

❹ Why do so many people try to avoid growing old? What is it they are afraid of?

❺ Think about how we are using our time on earth. Do humans do enough to help each other? Are there times when humans are very destructive? How might we make our lives more productive and meaningful?

❻ How might having a religious faith help people to cope with the fact that 'everything is constantly changing'?

Meditation

Meditation is a really important part of Buddhist life. The Buddha gained enlightenment through meditation and taught his followers to practise it regularly. It is one of the elements of the Noble Eightfold Path. There are many different types of meditation and this means that most people are able to practise a method which they are comfortable with. Meditation is meant to help focus your mind more carefully. It aims to help make the most of your life, to be able to see clearly what is useful and what is not. It's about being in control of your mind instead of it wandering aimlessly. If you are in control then you will be more aware of yourself and others around you.

IN THIS SECTION YOU WILL BE ASKED TO THINK ABOUT ...

✓ Determination
✓ Perseverance
✓ Training the mind
✓ Inner peace
✓ Coping with stress

stimulus 1 *The Buddha's enlightenment*

Prince Siddhatta left his father's palace as a young man to go in search of the answers to his questions about life. He was particularly concerned about the suffering he saw in the world outside the palace and he wanted to know how to help people who suffered. After years of searching and trying different religious practices, he eventually sat himself down under a sacred fig tree in the village of Bodhgaya, India. He adopted a cross-legged posture and vowed not to move from this position until he found the answers he was looking for. Everything around him became calm and peaceful. The birds made no noise and the trees stopped rustling in the wind. The Prince was determined to succeed in his quest but it wasn't to be easy.

First he had to defeat the evil Mara, his three sons Flurry, Gaiety and Sullen Pride and also his daughters Discontent, Delight and Thirst. Mara tried to control the mind of the young Prince. He and his children tempted and tormented Siddhatta in an effort to make him give up. But nothing they did could distract Siddhatta, so great was his determination to succeed. He stayed calm and unperturbed by the evil demon and his offspring. He put himself into a deep trance which lasted throughout the whole night. Buddhists nowadays call this the Four Watches.

In the first watch Siddhatta recalled all his previous births. He realised that he had been on earth many times before and this made him think about the whole process of birth, death and rebirth. He thought about how people must constantly leave behind those they love and be reborn to start again elsewhere. He saw the world and life within it going round and round like a wheel. In the second watch he understood that the kind of rebirth a person has depends on whether they have lived a good or a bad life. He realised that death is unpredictable and that we must do the best we can with our time on earth. His compassion towards others grew and grew as he understood more and more about life. In the third watch he meditated on the real nature of the world. He saw clearly that we are all bound by the cycle of birth, death and rebirth through ignorance. It seemed obvious that the way to stop the cycle is to stop the ignorance. This insight was the answer the Prince had been looking for. In order to help people with their suffering he had to help them gain knowledge about the source of the suffering and how to overcome it! As he entered the fourth watch of the night, dawn broke and the Prince became enlightened. He achieved Buddhahood. It was a most joyous moment for the world. Only Mara, who had been defeated, felt displeasure.

The Buddha remained in the same position under the bodhi tree for seven days. He was relaxed and comfortable without food and without sleep. He knew he had found fulfilment.

❶ Why had Prince Siddhatta left his father's palace? The stories in the unit on the Buddha's teaching will help you to answer this question.

❷ What position did he adopt when he sat under the fig tree? What vow did he make?

❸ Who is Mara? What was his role in the Buddha's enlightenment?

❹ Who were Mara's sons and daughters? What do you think they are meant to represent? In what ways do you think they tormented the young Prince?

❺ Make up your own symbols to represent Flurry, Gaiety, Sullen Pride, Discontent, Delight and Thirst. Use a dictionary to find the meaning of any of these words you don't understand.

❻ Suggest two reasons to explain why the Prince was not put off by the distraction which Mara tried to make.

❼ Stick four pictures of the Buddha meditating in your jotter. Make each picture represent one of the Four Watches. Draw a think bubble above the Buddha's head and write in the things which were going though his mind at each stage.

❽ According to the Buddha, what keeps us caught up in the cycle of birth, death and rebirth?

❾ Why do you think the Buddha's enlightenment is described as 'a most joyous moment for the world'?

❿ Imagine that you are the Buddha. Write a diary entry to explain how it is that you were able to go without food or sleep for so long. Describe how you feel to finally have the answers to your questions about suffering.

MAKING CONNECTIONS

❶ The Buddha was determined to achieve his goal. He left behind everything he owned in order to succeed. What is your goal in life? How do you aim to achieve that goal? Would you be willing to sacrifice lots of other things in your life in order to achieve your goal?

❷ Here are some different types of human suffering.

Physical pain   Sadness   Boredom   Confusion

Grief   Anger   Frustration   Jealousy

a) Which of them have you experienced?

b) Choose **one** experience of suffering that you clearly remember and work with a partner to role play a conversation with the Buddha. You should describe what happened to you, and your partner should be the Buddha listening, asking questions and trying to help you understand what caused the suffering and how you might cope better next time a similar situation arises.

stimulus

2 Extract from Maha Satipatthana Sutta (Greater Discourse on Steadfast Mindfulness)

Thinking it over

❶ The Buddha found all the answers to his questions within himself. He just needed to sit down and concentrate on the problems for long enough and the solutions came to him. Do you think this is a good way of solving problems? What does the Buddha's method teach us about the potential which human beings have to solve problems?

❷ Do you agree that life is like a cycle of birth, death, rebirth? What evidence of this is there in the world around us? Collect pictures and write poems to make a class display about 'the circle of life'.

❸ Think about the words of the song 'The Circle of Life' from the movie *The Lion King*. Your teacher might be able to play the song for you or show you a short clip from the film. How do the words of the song relate to the Buddha's understanding of life? Which lines of the song provide a message which might help us to avoid some of the suffering in our world? Discuss the different types of people described in the last verse of the song. How might the Buddha explain the different experiences of suffering described? How could we help each other to 'soar to the stars'?

Here bhikkus, a bhikku having gone to the forest, or to the foot of a tree, or to an empty, solitary place; sits down cross-legged, keeping his body erect, and directs his mindfulness. Then only with keen mindfulness he breathes in and only with keen mindfulness he breathes out. Breathing in a long breath, he knows, 'I breathe in a long breath'; breathing out a long breath, he knows, 'I breathe out a long breath'; breathing in a short breath, he knows, 'I breathe in a short breath'; breathing out a short breath, he knows 'I breathe out a short breath'. 'Aware of the whole breath body, I shall breathe in', thus he trains himself; 'aware of the whole breath body, I shall breathe out', thus he trains himself. 'Calming the process of breathing, I shall breathe in', thus he trains himself; 'calming the process of breathing, I shall breathe out', thus he trains himself … And again, bhikkus, a bhikku while walking knows, 'I am walking'; while standing, he knows, 'I am standing'; while sitting, he knows, 'I am sitting'; while lying down he knows, 'I am lying down.' A bhikku should know whatever way his body is moving or placed.

FINDING OUT

❶ Who do you think the Buddha is referring to as 'bhikkus'?

❷ What do you think it means to be 'mindful'?

❸ What kind of places does the Buddha say are good for meditation? Can you suggest some reasons why these places might be suitable?

❹ Write out your own version of the Buddha's instructions on how to become more mindful of the body. Give instructions on awareness of breathing and awareness of posture. You could present your work in the form of a leaflet.

stimulus
3 *Some lay Buddhists tell us about their experience of meditation*

I lead a very busy life. My work is hectic. I leave home at 6.30 every morning and commute into the centre of London by Tube. It's not a peaceful start to the day by anyone's standards. My days are usually full of meetings and struggling to meet strict deadlines. It's hard for me to find real time to meditate and yet the stressful life I lead means I need it more than most! My Buddhist teacher suggested that I try some meditations which fit into my everyday routine. One meditation I have particularly begun to enjoy is one I do while washing the dishes after our evening meal. My aim is to concentrate fully on how the water feels on my hands, to see the beauty of the bubbles created by the washing up liquid and not let my mind wander off to any other topic. At first it was hard – I thought it didn't really take much concentration to wash the dishes. But the meditation involved doing everything quite slowly and carefully, really being aware of all my movements. Now I really enjoy it! It gives me time to clear my mind of all the hectic things going on throughout the day and it has shown me that when I concentrate fully on only one thing at a time I can get more out of completing even the simplest tasks. Things which can appear as boring old routines, have taken on a new meaning in my life.

Allan

Every morning I get up an hour before the rest of my family. It's my time! In the corner of our spare room I have set up a little Buddhist shrine for myself. It contains a statue of Lord Buddha, some incense, a couple of candles and a bell. These things help me in my meditation practice. Sometimes I play some music too. I have only been meditating for a few months but I already feel the benefits from that hour every morning. I start the day with a clear mind and am ready to focus on any decisions I have to make throughout the day. I work in a nursery and spend all day with two year olds. They often shout and scream and cry and argue with each other! Without my morning meditation I think I'd be shouting and crying too some days! The meditation helps me to concentrate on the positive aspects of the children I care for. It helps me to remember that they are just children – learning how to behave. I can focus on my love for them rather than their difficult behaviour and that helps me to resolve difficult situations in a positive, loving way without getting too annoyed at the children. Regular meditation is helping me to stay calm and enjoy my job a lot more than I used to.

Yela

I take a little bit of time to meditate every lunchtime. I do walking meditation! It's the best thing to help recharge my batteries during the working day. I go to the local park which is near my office and spend twenty minutes in absolute calm and tranquillity. I learned about this type of meditation during a visit to the Samye Ling centre last year. You basically just walk very, very slowly trying to concentrate on the very act of walking. I try to feel every single part of my foot making contact with the ground each time I take a step. At the same time I breathe deeply allowing the air to refresh my body and my mind. After twenty minutes of that and a healthy sandwich lunch I am full of energy for the afternoon. My colleagues tell me they have noticed a difference in my attitude since I started my lunch time meditation sessions. I no longer experience that mid-afternoon slump!

Karina

> I have tried lots of different types of meditation over the past few years. It really fascinates me. I am currently studying the art of Zen meditation at a local Buddhist centre. I go to a class every Tuesday evening and again on Saturday mornings. There's about a dozen of us who attend regularly. This type of meditation encourages us to focus on the present. It's difficult at times! We sit in the lotus position and concentrate on breathing deeply and slowly, keeping our eyes open. It's really hard not to drift off! My teacher told us the other day that in Zen Buddhist monasteries whenever a monk is seen to be falling asleep during meditation he is hit across the shoulders with a stick! It's meant to be helpful but I'm not so sure I'd see it that way.

Marcus

❺ Marcus says he is studying the art of Zen Buddhism. Do some research to find out more about Zen Buddhism.

❻ Make up a fact sheet about meditation. Include at least ten interesting facts for people who don't know anything about meditation. Use different colours and shapes to make each fact stand out.

❼ Make up an acrostic poem using the word meditation. Focus on the benefits of meditation in your poem.

❽ Why do some people find meditation difficult?

❾ List some of the different objects often used in meditation.

FINDING OUT

❶ Copy and complete the following table:

Name	When does this person meditate?	How does meditation help him/her?
Allan		
Yela		
Karina		
Marcus		

❷ Allan meditates while washing the dishes. What other 'boring old routines' could be easily turned into a meditation?

❸ Karina says that she spends twenty minutes of her lunchtime in 'absolute calm and tranquility'. What do you think this means? Why might this be important for her?

❹ Yela says that her daily meditation helps her to 'resolve difficult situations in a positive and loving way'. What do you think she means by this? How might she deal with a toddler having a tantrum?

MAKING CONNECTIONS

❶ Do you ever find it difficult to concentrate? How might meditation help you to improve your concentration?

❷ Think about your daily routine. When would be the best time for you to do some meditation? What sort of meditation would suit you best? Give reasons for your answer.

❸ What kind of places make you feel calm and peaceful? Why?

❹ Try to include ten minutes of absolute peace and quiet into every day for a week. Keep a diary of how well you managed this and what you liked/disliked about that time each day.

Thinking it over

❶ Do you think that life is too hectic for most people? Think particularly about the adults in your life – do they spend too much time working and rushing around? How and when do they relax? What would be the benefits if everyone took a little bit of time for meditation each day?

❷ Should meditation be built into the school day? How might it help improve concentration, discipline and exam results? What problems might it cause?

❸ Do we tend to spend more time thinking about the past, the present or the future? Discuss the advantages and disadvantages of spending time thinking about each of these. Why do you think Buddhists encourage us to think more about the present than the past or the future?

Some people use prayer beads to count the number of times they have chanted a mantra. The style of the beads might vary depending on the type of Buddhism being practised.

A bell is sometimes used to mark different stages in a meditation. It might be rung to highlight that the worshipper is moving on to a different focus.

This helps to motivate worshippers by reminding them of the origins of their meditation practice. A statue of the Buddha meditating can have a calming influence.

stimulus
4 Aids to meditation

Candles help to create a reflective mood which is just right for meditation. Sometimes the flame itself can become the focus for concentration.

Incense is burnt as a way of purifying the air in the room. Depending on the fragrance it might be used to calm the mind or to help make the person more alert. Many Buddhists believe that as the smoke from the incense spreads out so do good deeds and the positive effects of meditation.

Posture is important during meditation and a cushion is often used. Buddhists try to sit with the back straight whilst still remaining comfortable and relaxed. Meditation is not meant to be a painful process.

FINDING OUT

❶ What am I? Can you solve the clues to name the objects you might find on a Buddhist shrine?

a) I will help you to remember why meditation is important.

b) I am meant to be held in your hands, not worn around your neck!

c) I am useful in the dark!

d) I can help you sit still during meditation.

e) I burn without a flame and smell nice too.

f) I might stop you from falling asleep if you get too relaxed!

❷ There are nine important words from stimulus 3 contained in this word search. Can you find all nine words then use them to write a short paragraph about how the objects can help people to meditate?

O	A	H	D	D	U	B	C	R	U
N	L	D	P	O	S	T	U	R	E
N	O	I	H	S	U	C	V	B	E
M	I	H	N	D	D	U	B	E	R
A	M	S	O	C	A	N	D	L	E
N	E	D	A	R	E	S	A	L	H
T	D	A	I	L	S	N	L	B	E
R	B	E	U	T	A	T	S	P	H
A	A	B	R	U	S	M	R	E	A
N	O	I	T	A	T	I	D	E	M

❸ Create a design for your own meditation cushion. Try to find some traditional Buddhist designs to use.

❹ Ask your teacher to light some incense in your classroom. If possible try different fragrances and talk about the kind of mood each might create.

❺ Set up a Buddhist shrine in your classroom. If you can't get hold of the actual objects, use drawings and mount them on card so they stand up.

MAKING CONNECTIONS

❶ The objects on a Buddhist shrine are considered as sacred. This means that they are special and therefore looked after carefully. What is the most important object you own? Why is this thing so important to you? How do you look after it? How would you feel if this object was lost or damaged?

❷ Buddhists use lots of things to help them concentrate. What about you? How easy or difficult is it to stop your mind from wandering off? What kind of thoughts distract you?

❸ Try sitting on the floor cross-legged with your back straight. How long can you sit still for? Try to feel each different part of your body connecting with the floor and feel the breath going in and out of your body. Remember you're meant to be relaxed! Describe how it feels to be sitting in this position. What would make it easier?

❹ Find out if there is a Buddhist centre near you that you can visit and try out some meditation. If that's not possible you might be able to invite a meditation teacher into your school.

Meditation: questions and answers

Can anyone meditate?

Yes, as long as you are willing to practise. You don't need to be a Buddhist. You don't need any special place either, you can meditate in your own home, at work, in the park, absolutely anywhere!

How long does it take to become good at meditation?

That all depends what you mean by 'good'. Meditation is for your benefit only, so as long as you are getting something out of your meditation then you are doing a good job! That can happen even the first time you try a simple breathing meditation. However, meditation is like a form of exercise for the mind. Just like any other exercise if you practise more often you will become better at it. Your mind will be 'fitter' the more time you put in to practise.

So how much time should I spend on meditation?

Ten to fifteen minutes every day is enough to start off with. The important thing is to plan the meditation into your day and not to keep putting it off thinking that you will get round to it later.

Do you always feel good after meditation?

Mostly, once you have practised meditation for a while it's like getting into a lovely soothing warm bath. You complete the meditation feeling calm and ready for anything. However, some types of meditation can bring unpleasant thoughts and feelings to the surface and you might be uncomfortable with that. The important thing is not to stop meditating because of this but to focus on the unpleasant things and try to understand what is causing them. Then you can get rid of these forever. It's like trying to create a beautiful garden, you have to do the digging and weeding in order to make space for the flowers to grow!

What do you think is the best thing about meditation?

For me it's about making my mind clear and pure. I can focus on anything I need to without distractions. It makes me a more peaceful and contented person. I feel more loving towards others and make more effort to be compassionate. I don't worry about the future anymore. Meditation helps me to see that it's more important to concentrate on what's happening now and to make the most of every precious moment.

Do you have any advice for people thinking about doing some meditation?

Take it a wee bit at a time! Don't worry about being perfect, just try to enjoy it. Think of your mind as a precious jewel which is covered in dirt and dust. Meditation will help you to clear away the muck and let the jewel shine. On a practical level, keeping a journal can help. Then you can write about the types of meditation you enjoy most, what distracts you most often and the feelings you experience from meditation. Read over the diary regularly and decide what you need to change to get more from your meditation.

FINDING OUT

❶ Explain why meditation is described as 'exercise for the mind'.

❷ In Stimulus 5 meditation is described as

a) Polishing the dirt off a precious jewel.

b) Creating the right conditions for a beautiful garden to grow.

c) Relaxing in a lovely warm bath.

Which description do you think is best? Why? Can you think of any other ways to describe meditation? Draw a picture to illustrate your description.

❸ Read the following letter and write a suitable reply using information from this section.

Dear Sir/Madam

Recently I have been reading about the benefits of meditation. I think it would be a good thing for me to try, but I'm not sure how to begin. Can you give me some advice? What's the best way to benefit from meditation?

Yours sincerely

Mr I. Cantdoit

❹ Explain why meditation can bring benefits even to those who don't meditate.

Thinking it over

1 How important is it for people to feel peaceful and content? What is meant by 'stress'? What sort of problems can arise when people feel stressed out?

2 Having a clear mind can help us to solve problems quickly. What sorts of things prevent us from having a clear mind? What causes these things? If our mind is unable to think clearly is this usually our own fault or someone else's?

3 Meditation involves regular time and effort if you want to reap the rewards. What other things in life can be beneficial if you put in the necessary time and effort? Why is it important not to give up on new things too soon? How does it feel when you become good at something you couldn't do before?

4 Buddhists believe that the mind and the body work together and so it's important to keep both healthy. Do you agree? How can we keep our bodies healthy? How does regular physical exercise help to improve the mind?

5 Many famous entertainers have taken up meditation. What makes their lifestyle so stressful? Do you think some jobs are likely to be more stressful then others? How can we avoid getting too stressed? How could employers help their workers to avoid stress?

# Ordination

For Buddhist families ordination is a major celebration when someone decides to become a monk or a nun. In some countries young people join a monastery for just a short time, others take vows which they keep for the whole of their life. In this section you will read about the preparations that must be undertaken by those who want to become Buddhist monks and nuns. You will also find out more about the promises they must make at the ordination ceremony and how the lifestyle they lead helps them to keep those vows.

IN THIS SECTION YOU WILL BE ASKED TO THINK ABOUT ...

✓ Family and community
✓ Possessions
✓ Making and keeping promises
✓ Leaving home

stimulus 1 Extract from diary of Ko Nyan, a Buddhist monk in Thailand

I will never forget the day I became a true member of the Sangha. Now, after studying for three years and trying to live by the ten precepts, at last I feel my life is as it should be. The day started with my parents kindly presenting me with a set of robes and my alms bowl. I asked them to forgive me for any wrong I have done to them over the years. It was so important to have their blessing. They have been a great support to me and as I walked away from them towards my new family, I knew that they were proud of my decision. They will miss me but they know I will be safe and nurtured in my new life.

I am honoured to have the venerable Lama Brahm as my Preceptor, he is one of the most senior monks in the monastery. He agreed to be responsible for all aspects of my wellbeing as long as I continue as a monk. In return, I agreed to care for him as if he were my own father.

During the ceremony the other monks asked lots of questions, the same questions which have been asked of all those being ordained. They were designed to test my suitability for the monastic life and were repeated several times by different people. I was a bit nervous at this stage but answered each question carefully just as we had practised the day before. I was also given my new name and had my head shaved. At one point two senior monks asked if anyone else objected to my being admitted as a monk – I held my breath and waited! They were given three chances to speak. No one replied and at 3.26p.m. on Saturday 18th September 2004 I officially became a monk. The date and time are carefully recorded so that my seniority within the Sangha is clear to everyone.

My family and friends celebrated by bringing me gifts for my room. Later on, once all the excitement had died down, I gave them away to some youngsters who have been helping with repairs in the monastery.

FINDING OUT

❶ Why do you think Ko Nyan says his life is now 'as it should be'?

❷ How did his parents show they were happy with his decision to become a monk? Why do you think this is important to him?

❸ The Sangha is the community of Buddhist monks and nuns. Why do you think Ko Nyan calls the Sangha his 'new family'?

❹ What does it mean to be 'nurtured'? Why is it important for humans to be nurtured?

❺ What sort of questions would you ask someone to see if they were suitable for monastic life? Work with a partner to make a list of questions and answers and then act out that part of the ordination ceremony for your classmates.

❻ The rest of the Sangha must agree to accept the new monk. How is this shown in the ordination ceremony? Suggest some reasons why this is important.

❼ Explain why the ordination ceremony is considered a celebration.

❽ Design a congratulations card for Ko Nyan. Include a special prayer for his future as a Buddhist monk.

❾ Do you think Ko Nyan was right to give away the gifts from his family? Discuss this in a small group and feed back your ideas to the rest of the class.

❿ Ko Nyan has to wear special clothes as a member of the Sangha. Collect pictures of people in all different uniforms. Find out why the uniforms are necessary and about any symbols on the uniforms. Create a class display about uniforms.

MAKING CONNECTIONS

❶ Ko Nyan now belongs to the Sangha. Which groups do you belong to? Draw a spider diagram, putting your name in the centre and surrounding it with names of all the groups you belong to. What does it mean to 'belong'?

❷ The ordination ceremony is a celebration of a new stage in someone's life. What stages in your life are celebrated in a special way? Have you ever taken part in or been to see a special ceremony or celebration? Share your stories with the rest of the class.

Thinking it over

❶ It's not just monks and nuns who live in communities. Many people in our society live in a community, for example, members of the armed forces, pupils at boarding schools, students at university. What are the advantages and disadvantages of living away from your family? In what ways might the people you live with become a substitute family? Would you like to live in this kind of community?

❷ What does it mean to be part of a family? Does a family have to consist of biological parents and children? How might adults help to nurture children in their care? What things do children need to feel good about themselves? How can children help adults? What do you think makes a successful family?

The Ten Precepts

1 I will abstain from destroying any other living creature.

2 I will abstain from taking anything which is not given to me by another person.

3 I will abstain from sexual activity.

4 I will abstain from telling lies or saying things that might cause harm to others.

5 I will abstain from drinks or drugs which might damage my mind and body.

6 I will abstain from meals after midday.

7 I will abstain from any kind of dancing, singing or musical entertainment.

8 I will abstain from using perfume and cosmetics or dressing up in fancy clothes or jewellery.

9 I will abstain from sleeping on any high or luxurious bed.

10 I will abstain from handling money.

❶ What does it mean to 'abstain'?

❷ Copy and complete this table by rewriting the Ten Precepts in a positive way using the phrase 'I will…'.

Precepts which prevent harm to others	Precepts which help prevent distraction

❸ What sort of personal qualities would a monk need in order to keep these vows? Explain your suggestions.

❹ Which two of the Precepts might be the most difficult for Ko Nyan to keep as he begins his new life? Give reasons for your answer.

❺ Imagine you are a friend of Ko Nyan. Write him a letter suggesting some things he might do if he ever feels tempted to break any of the Ten Precepts.

❻ Complete this sentence: 'Keeping the Ten Precepts will make you a better person because …'

A monk's possessions

Ko Nyan suddenly realised how much his life was about to change

1 Describe the main differences between Ko Nyan's old life and his new one.

2 What are 'alms'? Why do Buddhist monks need an alms bowl?

3 Look again at the list of Ten Precepts. Why would monks need a water filter? Would this be necessary for Buddhist monks living in Britain?

4 Different types of Buddhist monks wear different colours of robes. Find out more about the different colours worn and what they represent.

5 Design a leaflet to be sent out to all new Buddhist monks: 'Becoming a Monk – what you will need'. Try to explain why it is important not to bring lots of other things with you to the monastery. You could link this up with what you learned about the Ten Precepts.

6 Discuss with a partner. What would you miss most if you left home and went to live in a monastery? Why? Share your ideas with the rest of the class.

MAKING CONNECTIONS

1 Sometimes people make New Year resolutions when they want to give up bad habits. Have you made any New Year resolutions? Did you manage to keep them? How easy or difficult is it to stop doing things which have become habits in your life?

2 What sort of rules guide your everyday life? Are there things you try not to do? Write your own personal list of precepts.

3 A vow is like a promise. Have you ever made a promise and broken it? What do you think you should do if you break a promise to someone? Has anyone ever broken a promise to you? How does it feel when other people let us down by breaking promises?

4 What are your most precious possessions? Choose six things and explain why they are special to you. How would you feel if you had to give up these things? Why do we often find it difficult when our favourite things get lost or destroyed? What can you tell about other people in your class from their lists of special things?

Thinking it over

❶ Lots of people in the UK die or get really ill because of alcohol, cigarettes or illegal drugs. Why do people who know the dangers still continue to take these things? Should these things be completely banned from our society? Is addiction a weakness or an illness? Can people stop themselves from becoming addicted?

❷ What sort of rules are necessary for a successful community? Are the Buddhist Precepts too strict? Would some of them be good rules for everyone to follow?

❸ Do we put too much emphasis on making and spending money in our society? Is there too much pressure on people to have lots of possessions? Do we own too many things that we don't even need? In what ways might our modern lifestyles be harmful to the planet? Could we make better use of our money?

❹ Monks and nuns are taught not to worry about how they look. To what extent are people in our society judged by their appearance? Are good looks important? What other things are important when judging people?

stimulus

4 The Buddha's advice to Sariputra

When the Buddha was alive monks did not live in monasteries like the ones we see around the world today. Men who became monks left their families and spent a great deal of time searching for deeper knowledge of the Buddha's teachings. They found food and shelter wherever they could, only staying in one place for a short time. Monasteries and communities of monks gradually began to get established because the rainy season made it difficult to travel around. This extract from Buddhist scriptures details some of the advice the Buddha himself gave to his followers.

The monk alert, rapt farer on the edge,
Should have no fear of these five fears:
Gadflies and stinging bees and things that creep,
Attacks of men and four-footed beasts.

Nor should he be afraid of others' views
When the great perils of them he hath seen;
So should the expert seeker overcome
All other troubles that may here befall.

When stricken by disease or hunger pangs,
Cold and excessive heat should he endure;
When stricken sore by them, that homeless man
Must stir up energy and strive with strength.

Let him not steal or him tell a lie,
Let him show amity to weak and strong;
And where he knows disquiet of the mind,
Let him expel that as dark Mara's gloom.

Nor must he fall prey to wrath and pride,
But digging up their roots, let him stay poised;
And, as he wrestles, let him overcome
All that is dear to him, all that repels.

With joy in what is lovely, wisdom-led,
Let him then put to flight these troubles here,
Conquer dislike for his lone lodging place,
Conquer the four that cause him discontent.

'Alack! What shall I eat, and where indeed?
How ill I've slept! Where shall I sleep today?'
Whosoe'er trains and leads the homeless life
Must oust these thoughts that lead to discontent.

Sutta Nipata 964–70
From Buddhist Scriptures translated by E Conze

Mara, the evil demon

❶ Why were the first Buddhist monks often referred to as 'homeless'?

❷ Write a shorter version of the passage. Produce your own list of advice for monks by choosing one key point from each verse. Illustrate each of your key points with a picture if you can.

❸ What do you think it means to 'stir up energy and strive with strength'?

❹ What is 'disquiet of the mind'?

❺ In what ways can 'wrath and pride' be bad for us?

❻ How easy is it to 'oust these thoughts that lead to discontent'?

❼ To survive as a Buddhist monk you needed to be a pretty special kind of person. Choose *three* of the following words and explain why the early Buddhist monks would require these personal qualities:

Courage   Stamina   Wisdom
    Patience   Humility

❽ Make a mask of Mara, the demon which Buddhists believe tempts people and troubles their minds. Work with a partner to make up a short sketch in which one of you is Mara and the other is a Buddhist monk trying not to be distracted.

❾ Write a week's supply of daily messages which would help to keep a new monk focused on their vows. Each message should be a short phrase which the monk could read and remember each day, for example, 'There is wisdom in the Truth, the one who tells lies is foolish!'

stimulus 5 *Visit to a Buddhist monastery*

Inside the Kagyu Samye Ling monastery and Tibetan Centre

Dear Parent/Guardian

As part of their RE course work this term, class 2G have been studying what it means to become a Buddhist monk. In order to help them learn more about life in a Buddhist monastery, I would like to take them on a visit to the Kagyu Samye Ling Tibetan Centre near Eskdalemuir in the Scottish Borders.

Samye Ling is the largest Buddhist centre in Great Britain and it has the only purpose-built Buddhist temple. The centre was established in 1967 by a young Buddhist monk who had escaped from Tibet. He came to Britain and studied in Oxford before being given the land on which to build a brand new temple. His vision of a complete centre where Buddhist teaching and Tibetan culture could be preserved is gradually coming to life. The temple has been completed for some years now and work has started on other areas of the centre. The Abbot and monks run courses for visitors and also do a great deal of work for the charity Rokpa. I have already visited several times and found it both a most fascinating and peaceful place.

During our visit the pupils will have the opportunity to observe monks and nuns praying in the temple and to interview a Buddhist monk. They will have a tour of the magnificent temple looking at the variety of symbols and special objects used in Buddhist worship.

In the grounds of the centre there are two items of particular interest which we will explore. Firstly the Butter Lamp House where thousands of candles are lit every day and secondly the giant Stupa, a special Buddhist symbol of peace.

This visit will be a valuable experience for all the pupils. I do hope that you will allow your child to participate.

Yours sincerely

I Steele

Principal teacher of RE

Kagyu Samye Ling is just one example of a Buddhist centre in Britain. Tibetan Buddhism is a particular branch of Buddhism. Other Buddhists belong to different schools of the religion. Throughout Britain there are centres representing Theravadin, Mahayana and Zen Buddhism. These centres cater for the needs of both monks and lay Buddhists living in Britain and play an important role in helping this religion to flourish in this part of the world.

FINDING OUT

❶ Imagine you are a member of class 2G. How would you explain Mrs Steele's plans to someone in another class?

❷ Make a list of the questions you might ask the Buddhist monk if you were to interview him. Be ready to explain why you think these questions are important.

❸ Log on to www.samyeling.org and find out more about this Buddhist centre. Choose one of these tasks to complete:

a) Make your own visitor booklet for Samye Ling. Include information about the aims of the centre as well as the activities and facilities there.

b) Make up an information sheet for the pupils in 2G, 'Helpful hints for your visit to Samye Ling'. Include information on the Five Golden Rules for the centre as well as advice on what to bring, how to behave in the temple and what to expect from the visit.

4 Mrs Steele says she found the centre both 'fascinating and peaceful'. What do you think it is about Samye Ling that made her feel this? Why is it important for a Buddhist centre to have a peaceful atmosphere?

5 Find out about Tibet. You could watch the film *Seven Years in Tibet*. Why did the monk who started Samye Ling have to escape from his own country? If you had to leave Scotland and go to live in Tibet how would your lifestyle change? How is the life of a Buddhist monk in Tibet different from that of a Buddhist monk in Scotland?

6 Buddhism is a religion which hopes to bring about more peace in the world. How might becoming a Buddhist monk help bring about more peace?

7 In and around Buddhist temples there are many symbols of peace. Design your own peace symbol and make a display of these in your classroom.

8 Ask your teacher to arrange a visit to Samye Ling or another Buddhist centre near where you live. If this isn't possible, perhaps you could invite a Buddhist monk to visit you or use email to ask your questions.

Buddhists aim to build a Peace Pagoda in every country in the world. They hope this will spread blessings throughout the world and help to bring more peace into our lives. This one is in Battersea Park in London

If you don't have easy access to the Internet, you can get information by writing to Samye Ling at:
Kagyu Samye Ling Monastery and Tibetan Centre
Eskdalemuir
Langholm
Dumfriesshire
DG13 0QL

Thinking it over

❶ Imagine having to escape from your own country. What difficulties might you face settling in to a new and very different way of life? How could the people in that country help you?

❷ Should we allow asylum seekers to enter the UK? How are asylum seekers treated? What should the government do for these people? What can communities do to make new people feel more at home?

❸ Ask your teacher to find some news stories about refugees or asylum seekers. Read and discuss the stories. Why have these people left their own country? Should they be made to return? What's the best way to help them?

❹ Do you think enough is being done to make the world a more peaceful place? What might you personally do to bring a little more peace into the world?

stimulus

6 The Buddhists of Eskdalemuir

Ani Chudrun sits in the dining-room, her prayer beads playing between her fingers as she talks. It is the last meal of the day: soup, bread and whatever salad and vegetables are left over from lunch. Ani Chudrun is accustomed to media attention. As Beki Adam, she used to present the BBC television motoring programme, Top Gear. 'It was the classic Eighties lifestyle,' she remembers. 'Ambition, money, fast cars.'

The turning point came on camera, presenting an item about the Chevrolet Corvette. 'I asked the man, "From an environmental point of view," and he gave me an odd look and said, "Well, it's a strange thing to ask about a sports car." And I thought, well that's the end of that.'

She arrived at Samye Ling in 1993, and 'I immediately knew – I'm home. There was a whole community of people who felt exactly the way I did.' Her first year was fraught with difficulty. 'I was very angry all the time. I had a lot of things from the past weighing on my mind that I had to work through.' There was a flurry of press interest when she was ordained – 'TV Girl Beki Changes Gear'. She kept the press-clippings in a chest of drawers in her room, along with photographs and letters, mementos of her earlier life.

One day she left a candle burning on the shrine in her room. It caused a fire, which destroyed the chest of drawers, the press-clippings and the letters. 'I was distraught, and everybody else

Lama Yeshe

was sympathetic, but Lama Yeshe came up to me next morning and simply said, "You sort your head out," and walked off. It was just the most accurate and compassionate thing that

anybody could have said.' At the end of her first year, she took vows for a further three. Now she has taken vows for life.

Around us, plates are cleared, tables wiped clean. For the next hour and a half there will be prayer, the last of the day. By 9p.m. the monastery is silent. The beads click between Ani Chudrun's fingers.

Being a nun, she says, is like being in a relationship. 'You can do a year without properly giving yourself to it, in the knowledge that you can walk out if you want to. When it came to taking life vows it was like the prospect of marriage. I had this little voice in my head saying, "No, no, I want my freedom." But it was just my ego talking. Right after I'd taken life vows I felt joyously, shiningly happy.'

She smiles to herself. 'After I'd taken the vows, I asked the lama who had given them to me, "This is just for one life, isn't it?" I didn't want to get myself into anything that goes beyond that. But he said, the vows finish when your body finishes. That put it into perspective for me: it's just one life. That's not so long, is it?'

The Telegraph: 4th October 1997

FINDING OUT

❶ Choose one of the following tasks:

a) Use the information about Ani Chudrun to write your own newspaper article entitled: 'TV Girl Beki Changes Gear'. Describe her life before becoming a Buddhist nun and explain why she decided to change her lifestyle.

b) Imagine you are Ani Chudrun. Write a letter to your parents describing your new life at Samye Ling and explaining why you have made this huge decision.

❷ Ani says that when she arrived at Samye Ling she felt 'at home'. What do you think she meant by this?

❸ What difficulties did she experience during her first year as a nun?

❹ Do you think she was right to keep all the press clippings about herself? Give a reason for your answer.

❺ How did Lama Yeshe help after the fire destroyed her things?

❻ In what ways might becoming a monk or nun for life be like a marriage?

❼ After taking her vows, Ani Chudrun asked the lama 'This is just for one life isn't it?' What does this tell us about Buddhist beliefs?

❽ Imagine one of your friends was going to become a Buddhist monk or nun. What advice would you give? Explain your answer with reasons.

MAKING CONNECTIONS

❶ When you are older you will probably leave home and start a new stage in your life. Think about this and make two lists:

Leaving home	
Things I'm looking forward to	Things I'm a bit worried about

Discuss your lists in a small group and try to give each other some advice about the things that worry you about leaving home.

❷ What experiences make you really happy in life? Write about a time when your felt 'joyously, shiningly happy'. Was your happiness connected to money, people or something else?

Thinking it over

❶ Do you feel a part of a community where you live? How well do people know each other? How much do people care about each other? Have we become too concerned with our own individual lives to care much about others? What might you do to contribute more to the community you live in?

❷ Do you think people really understand what it means to be committed to something? Do we give up too easily these days? How can we show commitment to other people?

❸ Are people who become monks and nuns just taking an easy option by cutting themselves off from the real world? Is it more difficult to have a job and look after a family? Is the lifestyle they promote unrealistic for most of us? Could some of their ideas be helpful to the rest of us in our daily life?

 # *Karuna*

aruna is the Buddhist term for compassion. Compassion involves genuine feelings of pity and sadness when others are suffering in some way. If you feel compassion it means that you really feel sorry for another person and you want to do something to help them. To show compassion you must actually get involved in helping other people. The Buddha taught that compassion is the way to heal a great deal of the suffering in the world. If we all were able to show compassion to others then the links between all human beings would be stronger. To be compassionate means not thinking about whether you know or like the person who needs your help, but to have a genuine desire to stop the suffering felt by the person simply because they need your help. Nothing else counts!

IN THIS SECTION YOU WILL BE ASKED TO THINK ABOUT ...

✓ Compassion

✓ Wisdom

✓ Humanity

✓ Charity

✓ Prayer

 stimulus 1

Global Compassion: His Holiness the Dalai Lama

I believe that at every level of society – familial, national, and international – the key to a happier and more successful world is the growth of compassion. We all share an identical need for love, and on the basis of this commonality, it is possible to feel that anybody we meet, in whatever circumstances, is a brother or sister. No matter how new the face or how different the dress or behaviour, there is no significant division between us and other people. It is foolish to dwell on external differences because our basic natures are the same. The benefits of transcending such superficial differences become clear when we look at our global situation. Ultimately humanity is one and this small planet is our only home. If we are to protect this home of ours, each of us needs to experience a vivid sense of universal altruism and compassion.

FINDING OUT

❶ Who is the Dalai Lama? Why is he important to Buddhists? Do some research and produce a biography of the Dalai Lama. You could present your work in the form of a timeline or as a poster, booklet or news article.
The following websites will help you with this task:
• www.tibet.com
• www.nobelprize.org
You could also search the Internet for other sites with information about the Dalai Lama.

❷ Find out where Tibet is on a map. What sort of lives do the people there have? What is Tibetan Buddhism like?

❸ What do you think the Dalai Lama means when he says we should 'transcend such superficial differences'?

❹ What is meant by the term 'universal altruism'? Do you think it is possible to achieve this goal?

❺ What is the Dalai Lama asking humans to do? Make up a list of rules for humans based on the extract from his speech about global compassion.

❻ Collect pictures of people from all different nationalities and use them to illustrate the Dalai Lama's view that we are all brothers and sisters. You could make a poster entitled 'One Human Family' or 'Humanity is One'.

MAKING CONNECTIONS

❶ How can we be more compassionate to others? Copy and complete this table by giving another example of what you personally might do:

How can I be more compassionate:	
To my family?	1 Spend time with someone who is sad. 2
To other people in my community?	1 Raise money to help a local charity. 2
To people in other parts of the world?	1 Take part in a protest. 2

❷ Have you ever done something to help people you didn't know? Why did you do this? What difference do you think your actions have made? Did this change the way you feel about yourself in any way?

❸ What are the most important things in your life? What do you think we need most in order to be happy? Are material possessions more or less important than the people in your life? Give reasons for your answer.

❹ Look though some recent newspapers. Find articles which agree or disagree with the Dalai Lama's message.

❺ How would the news be different if we were a more compassionate society? Make up some news headlines which illustrate compassion in relation to the following issues:
a) Racist abuse
b) Asylum seekers
c) World poverty
d) Treatment of animals in zoos
e) Homelessness

❻ Have you ever been to an event which involved people from different parts of the world? What was the purpose of the event? Did you meet people from other countries? What was the atmosphere like?

❼ Try to get in touch with children from another country. Perhaps your teacher can help you to set up an e-mail link with another school. Try to discover what you have in common with those children.

❽ Plan a school assembly based on the theme 'One Human Family'. Write your own poems and/or songs to put across the message to the rest of your school.

Thinking it over

❶ The Dalai Lama thinks the key to a better world is compassion. What do you think about this idea? How do you think we can create a better world?

❷ Do humans do enough to protect the planet? Do you think we really do treat it as our only home? Give reasons for your answer. Make a leaflet encouraging others to protect the planet.

❸ Do you agree with the Dalai Lama that we are all part of the same human family? What do we have in common with those who live in different parts of the world? How can people from all over the world be helped to understand each other better? What can individuals and governments do to make it easier for us to help each other?

stimulus 2

ROKPA INTERNATIONAL

Rokpa is the Tibetan word meaning 'to help' or 'to serve'. ROKPA INTERNATIONAL is a charity organisation which was set up in 1980 by Dr Akong Rinpoche, the Tibetan doctor and Lama who created the Samye Ling Tibetan Centre in Scotland, along with the Swiss actress Lea Wyler and her father, the lawyer Dr Veit Wyler. ROKPA works in many countries around the world, always being true to its own motto 'Helping Where Help Is Needed'.

The flames illustrate the continual growth of ROKPA's work across the world and the increase of compassion, represented by the pure water.

The jewels represent the work which ROKPA volunteers do for people. Providing food for the hungry, homes for the homeless, medical help where it's needed, environmental work, education and counselling help for those suffering emotional distress.

This fruit is known as the aura plum, king of medicines. It is a reminder of the healing work which ROKPA tries to promote.

The Tibetan book represents the wisdom which ROKPA aims to nurture and to have as the foundation for all its activities. It aims to help others to develop wisdom through meditation and study. ROKPA aims for the unity of wisdom and compassion in all its activities.

ROKPA
Helping Where Help Is Needed

1 What is Rokpa International? What kind of work does Rokpa do?

2 Draw or trace the Rokpa logo and explain the symbols within it.

3 In what ways do Rokpa volunteers show compassion to others in the world?

4 Find out more about Rokpa by logging on to www.rokpa.org and produce a report about this important charity. Make sure you include information about:
a) How Rokpa began.
b) The countries that Rokpa works in.
c) Examples of the projects that Rokpa does.

5 Design a new Rokpa logo. Try to think of a design which communicates the compassion that Rokpa volunteers show.

6 Imagine that you are a volunteer on one of Rokpa's projects. Write a letter home describing the work you have been doing to your family. Try to describe the conditions for the people you have been helping and how the work has made you feel.

7 Create an advert asking for Rokpa volunteers. Include a list of the personal qualities you think the volunteers need to have.

MAKING CONNECTIONS

1 The Rokpa motto is 'Helping Where Help is Needed'. Where is help needed in your community? What kind of projects could Rokpa set up to help people near you?

2 Which charities do work in your area? Have you ever helped out with a local charitable event? Try to find out about volunteering in your community. Would you want to be a volunteer for an organisation like Rokpa? Give reasons for your answer.

3 Make a list of the ways in which your life is different from the children living with Rokpa in the Kathmandu orphanage. What might you have in common with them?

Thinking it over

1 Buddhism teaches that you need wisdom in order to be truly compassionate. Do you agree? What might happen if you tried to help someone without thinking it through first? How would you define 'wisdom'?

2 Is it right that so many people in our world rely on charity to help them survive? Are there any alternatives?

3 'Everyone who has a job should give a small percentage of their wages to help others less fortunate.' Do you agree or disagree with this statement? Give reasons for your answer.

stimulus
3

A Buddhist story about compassion

This is a story from the *Jataka Tales*, a collection of stories about the Buddha's birth and his previous lives. The story illustrates the greatest kind of compassion.

Two monks are on a pilgrimage trekking through the jungle of northern India.

They come across a lioness in a cave who has recently given birth to five or six cubs. The lioness is very hungry and weak.

The lioness is so desperate for food that she is considering eating the youngsters she has just given birth to. The monks are horrified by this idea.

One of the monks go off to search for some food for the lioness while the other stays with the lioness and her cubs.

Left alone with the starving animals the monk begins to think things through.

The monk throws himself from the top of the cave and the lioness begins to feast.

The other monk returns having found no meat elsewhere.

FINDING OUT

❶ What is a pilgrimage? In what ways might a pilgrimage 'focus the mind'?

❷ The monks were horrified by the thought of the lioness eating her own cubs. Why would this seem such a terrible thing?

❸ How did the monks in the story show their compassion?

❹ Write a modern newspaper version of this story. It doesn't have to be animals that are saved.

❺ Which of the following words do you think best describes the monk who gave his life?

Stupid   Selfish   Loving   Insane

Give a reason to explain your choice.

❻ Try to watch part of the movie *Seven Years in Tibet*. Find out what happened to the worms when the monks were asked to dig the earth and lay foundations for the Dalai Lama's cinema.

MAKING CONNECTIONS

❶ The monk in the story gave his life as a sacrifice. What is a sacrifice? Have you ever sacrificed anything of your own in order to help others?

❷ The story illustrates the Buddhist teaching about equality between animals and humans. What are your views on animal rights? Are humans and animals equal?

❸ Read this short newspaper extract:

Teacher saves pupils in gun attack on school

Yesterday in Mayflower High School, Pennsylvania, a young male teacher stepped in front of two small children in order to save them from a crazed gunman. Philip Munch lost his life in the process. As soon as he moved to protect the youngster, the gunman, who had entered the school building by posing as a parent, opened fire and delivered two fatal shots to Philip's stomach and neck. The children's parents have praised him for his brave act of compassion.

a) In what ways is this similar to or different from the story of the Buddhist monks?

b) Do you think Philip Munch should be honoured for his actions?

c) Why might this be described as an act of compassion? Do you know of other stories about people who have acted like Philip Munch?

4 *Bodhisattvas*

In Mahayana Buddhism people believe in the existence of special beings called Bodhisattvas. A Bodhisattva is someone who has decided to delay entry into the final enlightenment in order to spend more time helping others. Instead of leaving this world at death, the Bodhisattva may return as many times as he or she likes in order to spread loving kindness and help others along the path to enlightenment. The Buddha was considered to be a Bodhisattva in his previous lives before being born as Gotama.

Avalokitesvara

Avalokitesvara is a Bodhisattva who is often called 'The One Who Looks Down'. He is famous for being compassionate to all those who need help. Tibetan Buddhists believe that the Dalai Lama is a reincarnation of this Bodhisattva. Buddhists pray to Avalokitesvara for help in their daily life.

In order to help as many people as possible in all different situations, the Bodhisattvas can change into any shape or form. These different forms are called *incarnations* of the original. Buddhists say that Avalokitesvara has made more incarnations than any other Bodhisattva. In China the Bodhisattva is believed to take a female form and is known as Kuan-yin, 'The One Who Takes Notice of the Cries of the World'. The story of her life shows how compassionate she is believed to be:

Born into a royal family, when she was a young girl Kuan-yin was the perfect daughter. She was kind to her servants, kind to her parents and indeed quite charming to all those who came into contact with her. Her only desire was in helping others. She showed no interest in the life of her family or in being married and having children of her own to continue the family line. This concerned her father greatly and he tried hard to persuade her otherwise. Instead she begged him to allow her to leave home and follow a religious life and eventually he gave in. However, he banished her from his home vowing never to see her again.

One day the King fell ill, doctors were called but could do nothing. The royal physician declared that in order to produce the medicine the King needed he must have the eyes and arms of one who had showed no anger ever in their life. The King could think of no one but one of his advisers informed him of a Bodhisattva living in the north of the country who had a reputation for this type of personality and great kindness to all beings. A messenger was dispatched and when faced with the request, the Bodhisattva showed no hesitation in removing her eyes and severing her arms. She happily gave them to save the King's life. When the king recovered he and his wife went to thank the Bodhisattva. On discovering it was his daughter, he moved forward to lick her wounds and hold her in his arms but alas, it was too late, the gods came down and took her to the heavens at that very moment.

❶ What is a Bodhisattva?

❷ Why is the Bodhisattva Avalokitesvara so special?

❸ What does the term 'incarnation' mean? Why would a Bodhisattva take on different incarnations?

❹ Look closely at the picture of Avalokitesvara. What symbols can you identify in the picture? How have Buddhists tried to illustrate that he represents supreme loving kindness to all beings on earth?

❺ Suggest two reasons why Buddhists think that the Dalai Lama might be an incarnation of Avalokitesvara. What do they have in common?

❻ What do the Chinese call Avalokitesvara?

❼ The Bodhisattva's Chinese name means 'The One Who Takes Notice Of The Cries of the World'. What do you think the 'cries of the world' might be? Make a collage of news stories and pictures to illustrate this theme.

❽ Look back at the section on the Buddha's teaching. What similarities are there between the Buddha's life story and that of Kuan-yin?

❾ Produce your own storyboard of the story of Kuan-yin. Include speech and think bubbles to show clearly how different characters felt at different times in the story.

❿ Why do you think her father was reluctant to allow her to take up a religious life? Was he right to let her go eventually? Give reasons for your answer.

⓫ Buddhists pray to Avalokitesvara for help in their daily life. What might people ask for help with? Make up your own Buddhist prayer. Draw a border around your prayer and decorate it to make it look like a page of a holy book.

⓬ Conduct a class survey to find out peoples' attitudes to prayer.

⓭ Invent your own Bodhisattva and write a story of how the Bodhisattva helps someone suffering in the modern world.

Thinking it over

❶ What are the advantages and disadvantages of believing in Bodhisattvas?

❷ If you were able to take on a different form or 'incarnation' what would you like to be and why? In what ways might you be able to do more good in the world if you were able to change your shape and form as you liked?

❸ What is the point of prayer? Have you ever prayed for help? How did it make you feel? Do you think your prayers were answered? Why/why not? Is it better to pray for yourself or to pray for others?

❹ Do you think it will ever be possible to rid the world of misery? Why/why not? How can we as humans help to achieve this?

Prayer wheels and compassion

Child: I went on a school trip to a Buddhist temple and saw some objects called prayer wheels. What are they for?

Monk: Buddhists believe that using a prayer wheel is an act of compassion. Each time the wheel is turned the prayers are sent out to reduce the suffering of all beings in the world. The more times the wheel is turned, the more prayers are sent out into the world.

Child: The prayer wheels I saw were of different shapes and sizes. Why is that?

Monk: Some prayer wheels are small so people can hold them and carry them around with them. Others are large and contain millions of mantras. These are designed to be placed in and around temples so that visitors can turn them as part of their worship. You can see some of the different types in these pictures.

Child: So, prayer wheels come in many different shapes and sizes but they all contain a number of prayers or mantras within the drum. How many prayers are inside the wheel will depend on how big the wheel is, is that right?

Monk: Yes that's right but there is one prayer which is more popular than others; it is the famous Buddhist mantra 'Om Mani Padne Hum'. This mantra is to be found inscribed on the outside of many prayer wheels as well as being contained within them. Some Buddhists believe that even

seeing the mantra can bring feelings of joy and reduce suffering.

Child: Why is this prayer so special?

Monk: This particular prayer is considered to be a call to the Bodhisattva Avalokitesvara. Tibetan Buddhists in particular believe that if this mantra is spoken out loud or even in silence to oneself, then the Bodhisattva will come and offer help in some shape or form.

Om Mani Padne Hum in Tibetan script

Child: I've heard of that Bodhisattva. Does the prayer work for anyone or do you need to be Buddhist?

Monk: Buddhists believe in showing compassion to anyone who is in need of it. So anyone can benefit from the Bodhisattva. Whenever you find yourself with a problem or experiencing pain of any kind, all you have to do is repeat the mantra 'Om Mani Padne Hum' and help will come.

Child: That's cool! I'll try that next time I'm in trouble.

Monk: Buddhists don't usually wait until they personally need help though, the mantra is recited everyday by millions of Buddhists all over the world and millions of prayer wheels containing the mantra are spun everyday. In this way Buddhists hope that all those who are suffering will be helped.

Child: That means that you are trying to help anyone and everyone, even if you don't know who they are or what they are suffering from.

Monk: Yes indeed! That's true compassion my child; not to be concerned about yourself but to show concern for others without caring about any reward for yourself. That's the meaning of altruism.

Child: Sounds really great! Maybe if we all practised a bit more altruism the world would be a better place… with the Bodhisattva's help too of course!

FINDING OUT

❶ What is a prayer wheel? Why are there different types of prayer wheels? How do Buddhists use them?

❷ Design and draw or make your own prayer wheel.

❸ Sometimes Buddhists write the mantra 'Om Mani Padne Hum' on stones which they keep in their pockets or leave lying around for people to see. Draw your own mantra stone using the language above. Explain why this mantra is so important to Buddhists.

❹ Ask your teacher to find a recording of a Buddhist monk chanting the mantra and listen to it carefully. Do you think it sounds like a prayer? Repeat it to yourself several times. How do you think it would feel to repeat this lots of times everyday?

❺ As well as prayer wheels, Buddhists also use prayer flags to send prayers out across the world. Find out what prayer flags look like. Get everyone in your class to make a flag with a prayer for suffering people on it. String them up and display them in your classroom.

❻ What do Buddhists think about non-Buddhists using prayer wheels? Suggest two reasons for this viewpoint.

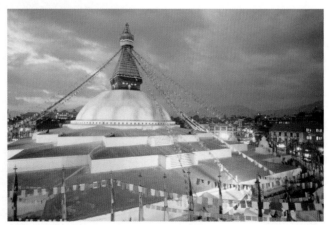

Prayer flags in Kathmandu, Nepal

MAKING CONNECTIONS

❶ What is the kindest thing you have ever done for anyone? Write a diary entry of your actions and describe the outcome.

❷ Who is the kindest person you know? Write a magazine article about this person describing some of the acts of kindness they have performed for you and for others.

❸ A mantra is like a motto for your life. It motivates and inspires you every day. Make up your own motto for life. Explain how this motto will help you through both good and bad days. Design a symbol to go with your mantra.

❹ 'If you repeat something often enough inside your head you will start to believe it no matter what'. Do you agree? Have you ever repeated a phrase over and over in order to help keep yourself positive about something, for example, 'I can pass this test, I can pass this test, I can pass this test...' Did your repetition work?

❺ Some Buddhists think of Bodhisattvas like a kind of guardian angel looking after them. Have you ever felt that there was someone or something spiritual which is looking after you? How might this kind of belief help people who are going through a difficult time in life?

Thinking it over

❶ If I do my gran's shopping she gives me some pocket money.

I love my gran a lot. She always tries to give me money but I couldn't take it!

Which viewpoint do you think is more correct? Should we expect a reward for helping people? What if everyone expected a reward? If you accept a reward does that mean the help you gave is worth less? Is it possible to feel rewarded without actually having received anything from the person you helped?

❷ Should we ask for help when we have problems or try to fix them for ourselves? Is prayer an easy answer to our difficulties?

❸ 'People often give up too easily. Working through your problems makes you a stronger person.' Do you agree or disagree? Give reasons for your answer.

❹ How might altruism help to create a stronger sense of humanity? Could the Buddhist teachings about Karuna work in our modern world? Is it realistic to expect people to help those they don't even know? What are the positive and negative aspects of this?

Christianity

Agape

This unit explores Christian ideas about love especially 'agape', the Greek word for love in action or practical love. It includes passages from the Bible which show examples and teaching about agape love from the life of Jesus and the first Christians. It also looks at two organisations today, Christian Aid and The Salvation Army, which show agape love in action.

IN THIS SECTION YOU WILL BE ASKED TO THINK ABOUT ...

✓ Love

✓ Sharing

✓ Fairness

✓ Quality of life

 1 ## The Bible on love

Love is a difficult word because it can have so many different meanings.

```
C:/Sign on
Enter: <Bible>
C:/ User password
Enter: <God's Word>
C:/ System Access 00:00:01
C:/ Search<Love>
File found: Storge
File found: Phileo
File found: Eros
File found: Agape
C:/ Run:: <Storge>
> File: family love; binds families together
C:/ Run:: <Phileo>
> File: friendship – binds groups together
C:/ Run::<Eros>
> Access denied
C:// Search: <Eros>
> Access restricted:// contact system
administrator
C:/Run Eros: <password ****>
>File: romantic or sexual love
[00:00:10 prohibited – exceeds the DDR
count of prohibited or questionable words]
C:/ Run <Agape>
>File: charity, giving, love in action, practical
love
```

```
C://Search: <Agape in 21st Century>
>File: Christian Aid, TEAR Fund..........
<File Interrupt: 00:00:10 Data exceeds
capacity:
>>>System closing>>>>00:00:20
>>>Strike any key to restart>>>>>
```

❶ What four words did the computer give for love?

❷ Why do you think the search for Eros was 'prohibited'?

❸ What meanings are given for the word agape?

❹ What Christian organisations are suggested which put agape love into practice?

❺ What other Christian organisations do you know which put agape love into practice? Use the Internet to help you and display your findings in class.

MAKING CONNECTIONS

❶ Think about the four words for love in Stimulus 1. Which are linked with the following? (NB Some may be linked with more than one.)
a) Brothers and sisters.
b) Best friends.
c) Mother and daughter.
d) Husband and wife.
e) Looking after an elderly relative.
f) Doing volunteer work for a local charity.

❷ Listen to a recent song about love and in groups discuss the words. What kinds of love are being described?

❸ What or who do you love? Match each of your answers to one of the four words for love. What does your answer tell you about yourself and what you value?

 stimulus 2 *Paul's teaching on love*

The passage below is about love and is often read at weddings. A Christian called Paul wrote it. It is found in a letter he wrote to Christians in Corinth.

> *Love is patient and kind;*
> *Love is not jealous or conceited or proud;*
> *Love is not ill-mannered or selfish or irritable;*
> *Love does not keep a record of wrongs;*
> *Love is not happy with evil, but is happy with the truth;*
> *Love never gives up; and its faith, hope and patience never fail.*
>
> *Meanwhile these three remain: faith, hope and love; and the greatest of these is love.*

Paul's first letter to the Corinthians, 13:4–7;13

 FINDING OUT

❶ Which of the four meanings of love is Paul describing in his letter to the Corinthians?

❷ Make two lists based on the passage from Paul's letter. In the first, write down what love is and what it does; in the second list, write down what love is not and what love does not do.

MAKING CONNECTIONS

❶ Describe a time when someone was patient or kind towards you. How did it make you feel?

❷ Describe a time when you were grumpy, selfish or irritable. What happened as a result? How did you feel afterwards?

❸ Choose one of the statements in Paul's letter about what love is and make up a modern day story to illustrate it.

❹ Write your own list starting 'Love is…'. Discuss your ideas with others in your group and design a group poster.

Thinking it over

❶ Look at the qualities of love in the passage. Which three do you think are the most important? Give reasons for your view.

❷ Paul claimed that 'Love never gives up'. Can people suddenly stop loving someone? Can people love someone and hurt them at the same time?

❸ 'Sometimes it is impossible to love others.' Do you agree or disagree?

❹ Should you only love those who love you? Why/why not?

❺ Discuss what is meant by faith and by hope. Do you agree that of faith, hope and love, love is the greatest? Why/why not?

❻ Do you think the passage is a good one to have at a wedding? Why/why not?

When the Son of Man comes in his glory, and all the angels with him, he will sit on his throne in heavenly glory. All the nations will be gathered before him, and he will separate the people one from another as a shepherd separates the sheep from the goats. He will put the sheep on his right and the goats on his left.

...

Then the King will say to those on his right, 'Come, you who are blessed by my Father; take your inheritance, the kingdom prepared for you since the creation of the world. For I was hungry and you gave me something to eat, I was thirsty and you gave me something to drink, I was a stranger and you invited me in, I needed clothes and you clothed me, I was sick and you looked after me, I was in prison and you came to visit me.'

...

Then he will say to those on his left, 'Depart from me, you who are cursed, into the eternal fire prepared for the devil and his angels. For I was hungry and you gave me nothing to eat, I was thirsty and you gave me nothing to drink, I was a stranger and you did not invite me in, I needed clothes and you did not clothe me, I was sick and in prison and you did not look after me.'

...

Then they will go away to eternal punishment, but the righteous to eternal life.

Matthew 25:31–46

stimulus 3

Love in action: Jesus' teaching

Jesus told a parable which taught that people who lived their lives according to his teaching would be with God. Those who didn't would go to Hell. In this parable he challenged people to think about how they showed love to people in need.

1 Read the extract from the parable of the sheep and the goats. Who did Jesus say would be 'with God'? Why would they be with God?

2 Look at the table below. Match up the kind of people Jesus was talking about with people in society today.

Who Jesus was talking about	People in society today
The hungry	Drought sufferers in the developing world
The naked	A drug addict
The thirsty	People living in poverty in Scotland
The stranger	A captured terrorist
The sick	People who are homeless
The prisoner	A refugee

3 Create a display in class which uses artwork to show the people Jesus was talking about in this teaching. Either use your own drawings or use a collage of images from newspapers and magazines.

stimulus

4 *Love in action: the first Christians*

Jesus said 'Love the Lord your God with all your heart, and with all your soul, and with all your strength, and with all your mind: and your neighbour as yourself' (Luke 10:25–7).

The first Christians tried to put this teaching into practice and made love for your neighbour a way of life. Many of them lived together in groups. The wealthy would sell all they had and share it among the others. There were no slaves – everyone was thought of as equal in the eyes of God. Everyone was expected to contribute to the group with their own skills. Everyone gave what they could and took what they needed. Love was not just an idea, it was something to be put into practice.

All the believers continued together in close fellowship and shared their belongings with one another. They would sell their property and possessions, and distribute the money among all, according to what each one needed. (Acts 2:43–5).

The group of believers was one in mind and heart. No one said that any of his belongings was his own, but they all shared with one another everything they had... There was no one in the group who was in need. Those who owned fields or houses would sell them, bring the money received from the sale, and hand it over to the apostles; and the money was distributed to each one according to his need.

And so it was that Joseph, a Levite born in Cyprus, sold a field he owned, brought the money, and handed it over to the apostles (Acts 4:32–7).

Copy and complete the paragraph by using the words below:

The first Christians followed the example of Jesus and put love into .... They sometimes lived together in .... and .... everything they had. They sold their .... and .... and distributed the money to those who needed it. Joseph, a .... from ...., sold his field, brought the money and gave it to the ....

property	poor	Levite	possessions
groups	action	Cyprus	shared

Thinking it over

❶ What do you think about the idea of people living in groups and sharing everything they have? What might be the advantages and disadvantages?

❷ Do you think people today should be prepared to sell their property and possessions and give the money to those who need it? Why/why not?

❸ Do you think it is OK for people to gain personally from helping others? (For example, young people who do voluntary work often gain new skills and experience that can help them get a better job later in life.)

❹ Should the definition of neighbour include anyone, no matter where they live or what their religion or nationality is? Give reasons for your answer.

❺ Do you think helping others will always be necessary? What makes you say that?

Love in action: Christian Aid

Christian Aid believes in strengthening people to find their own solutions to the problems they face. It strives for a new world transformed by an end to poverty and campaigns to change the rules that keep people poor.

Towards a new earth

Supported and sustained by the churches and driven by the Gospel, Christian Aid is inspired by the dream of a new earth where all people can secure a better and more just future. Christian Aid's purpose is to expose the scandal of poverty and to contribute to its eradication. Christian Aid recognises that change will only come about as a movement is built of individuals who are committed to a better world for all, bringing their faith and talents, their energy, their influence, their gifts and their actions, to achieve what should surely be possible. (www.christianaid.org.uk)

Prayer for a new earth

God of all places and this place:
you promised a new earth
where the hungry will feast and the
   oppressed go free.
Come Lord, build that place among us.

God of all times and this time:
you promised a new day
when the fearful will laugh
and the sick find healing.
Come Lord, speed that time among us.

God of all people, our God:
take what we have and what we hope for
make this a world where the poor find good
   news.
We come Lord, to share in the work of your
   Kingdom
until the new earth is created among us.

© *Christian Aid*

❶ What is Christian Aid's main purpose?

❷ How do they believe they will achieve this?

❸ Does Christian Aid only show love to other Christians? How do you know?

❹ Look at the Christian Aid prayer. Write down in your own words what sort of world is prayed for.

❺ Christian Aid works to help the poor and to challenge why they are poor. What is the difference? Give some examples.

❻ Look at the Christian Aid website www.christianaid.org.uk. Make up a fact sheet about their work.

MAKING CONNECTIONS

❶ What do you think 'good news' would be for the poor? Make up your own newspaper headline about good news for the poor.

❷ Christian Aid is always on the lookout for volunteers. Look at the fact sheet you produced from their website. What aspect of their work do you think you could contribute to?

❸ Christian Aid believes in making life good for people now. Choose one group in your local community, for example, OAPs, single mums with small children, or individuals looking after elderly relatives. What things do you think would make life better for them?

stimulus
6

Love in action: The Salvation Army

The Salvation Army is sometimes described as 'Christianity with its sleeves rolled up'. This is because it is so well known for putting Christian love into action – sometimes in very difficult circumstances. The Salvation Army is a worldwide organisation which works in many areas. On its website you will find that it does all kinds of work all over the world. Here in the UK it is one of the largest Social Services agencies there is. Here are some of the things it does in the UK.

Helps the homeless: There are hostels where the homeless can stay but there are also places which assess people so that they can get the best possible help according to their needs. There are also practical classes helping the homeless in everything from DIY skills to learning to read and write.

Provides Community Services: This could be day care for the elderly or those with special needs. It could be visiting people at home and doing simple things for them there. It might even be before and after school clubs for children. There are also services to help those who are disabled lead normal lives.

Provides care for children and families: There are four residential children's homes in the UK. This could be for emergency care where children are being abused or just to give families a break. Sometimes children who would be sleeping on the streets are brought there by the police. There is a also a refuge for women who are trying to escape violence in the home.

Helps prisoners: This involves prison visiting as well as trying to rehabilitate prisoners for their release through special programmes.

Gives help in emergencies: The Army responds to emergency situations as they arise providing food, emergency equipment and comfort and support. It also has a very well-developed programme for tracing missing persons.

Provides addiction services: The Army has always worked with those who are alcoholics or addicted to drugs. This involves treatment, support and guidance for substance abusers.

As well as all this, the Salvation Army works all over the world in many ways. To find out more about the incredible variety of work it carries out, including some things which might surprise and shock you, visit www.salvationarmy.org.uk.

FINDING OUT

❶ Why is The Salvation Army sometimes called 'Christianity with its sleeves rolled up'?

❷ What does it do to help the homeless?

❸ What kinds of things does it do to help children and families?

❹ How does it help the elderly?

❺ How does it help drug addicts and alcoholics?

❻ 'The Salvation Army tries to help people by providing them with skills to make a better life for themselves.' What evidence is there for this?

❼ Look up the Salvation Army website. Write down two other campaigns or activities the organisation is involved in.

Thinking it over

❶ In your opinion which of the activities of the Salvation Army is most helpful? Why?

❷ 'It's OK helping families and children, but the Salvation Army shouldn't help addicts and prisoners.' Why might some people argue this? Why would followers of the Salvation Army disagree with this? What do you think?

❸ Which statement is nearer your own view? Why?

> If more people showed love we wouldn't need organisations like the Salvation Army.

> Sadly, there will always be a need for organisations like the Salvation Army.

❹ What have you learnt about the meaning of love through your study of this topic?

Holy Communion

One of the most important practices within Christianity is Holy Communion. In some churches this is sometimes called the Eucharist or the Breaking of Bread. This unit focuses on the practices and the meaning of Holy Communion for Christians, and looks at the origin of this practice. The unit also looks at the lives of two famous Christians who followed the example of Jesus.

IN THIS SECTION YOU WILL BE ASKED TO THINK ABOUT ...

- ✓ Remembering
- ✓ Thanking
- ✓ Sharing
- ✓ Celebrating
- ✓ Sacrifice

stimulus 1 *The Last Supper*

The night before he died Jesus celebrated a meal with his disciples. It was his last meal with them. Below are two versions of this. The first is from the Bible and the second is a modern interpretation.

The disciples left, went to the city, and found everything just as Jesus had told them; and they prepared the Passover meal. When it was evening, Jesus came with the twelve disciples. While they were at the table eating, Jesus said, 'I tell you that one of you will betray me – one who is eating with me'. The disciples were upset and began to ask him, one after the other, 'Surely you don't mean me, do you?'

While they were eating, Jesus took a piece of bread, gave a prayer of thanks to God, and handed it to his disciples. 'Take it', he said, 'this is my body'.

Then he took a cup, gave thanks to God, and handed it to them; and they all drank from it. Jesus said, 'This is my blood which is poured out for many, my blood which sealed God's covenant. I tell you. I will never again drink this wine until the day I drink the new wine in the Kingdom of God.' (Mark 14:16–19,22–5)

Jesus met with his disciples one night for dinner. This was no ordinary dinner. Tonight he was about to tell them that he would soon die for them. He gathered his friends around him, including two he knew would betray him. But this wasn't the time for anger or sadness – their guilt would come later. He knew he had to leave them all, but he trusted that he would see them again after death. But would they believe it? He'd asked them before to believe some difficult things – but this was different. Wouldn't they just feel let down? Their bold leader who promised so much, would end up beaten and bowed – dying like a thief. Where would their trust in him be then?

How could he gently break the ending which must come soon? The bread, the wine, that was the way. Give them something to hold on to, something to share, something to do after he had gone which would remind them of his pains, but also his victories. They were Jews after all, they knew about the lamb which must be sacrificed for the good of all. He would be that lamb. That they would understand all right.

He held a rough-baked loaf: 'This is my body which will be broken for you. Take it, eat it.

A painting of 'The Last Supper' by Leonardo da Vinci

When you do that from now on remember me.' They took it and passed it round. They were puzzled. They'd work it out soon though. He lifted a cup of wine, deep red. 'This is my blood which will be shed for you. Drink, and when you do remember me.' They were getting a little nervous, asking questions. 'What did he mean?' 'How could that be?' 'What makes you think we'd let that happen?' But it would happen, and it would be dreadful. But it had to happen and it would be remembered. No, it would be celebrated...

❶ During the meal with his disciples what did Jesus say about being betrayed? How did his friends react? What does it mean to 'betray' someone?

❷ What did Jesus do with the bread and wine? What do you think he meant?

❸ What did Jesus say when he broke the bread? What do you think he meant?

❹ What did he say when he lifted the cup of wine? What did he mean?

❺ Use a dictionary to find out what is meant by the word 'covenant'.

❻ The bread and wine are symbols. What is a symbol and what do the words spoken about bread and wine and the actions symbolise?

❼ Why do you think the second passage describes the disciples as being 'a little nervous'?

❽ Imagine you were one of the disciples present at the last supper. Write about what you saw, did and felt.

❶ Imagine you are leaving to go to live in a new place. You want to meet with friends for the last time. How would you celebrate this event? What kind of things would you want to do? What would you say to them? What might they say to you? What could you do to help your friends remember the occasion?

❷ Have you ever felt let down by someone? Write about your experience.

❸ In groups, discuss ideas for a short story in which someone is betrayed. Each person in the group should write part of the story and then the group should meet up again to create the 'final' version.

Thinking it over

❶ The stimulus is headed 'The Last Supper'. Why?

❷ 'The last supper is about remembering.' What do you think Jesus wanted his disciples to remember about him?

❸ The last supper is about a group of friends meeting for the last time. Do you think the disciples were good friends of Jesus? Why/why not?

❹ Bread and wine were common everyday foods, eaten at most meals. If the last supper meal had been held today would Jesus have used bread and wine or chosen something else? What might he have chosen?

❺ Using the Internet, find some paintings of the Last Supper. What is each painting trying to say?

stimulus 2 *The practice of Holy Communion*

Holy Communion is the time when Christians meet together to re-enact the Last Supper and remember the actions of Jesus. Different churches celebrate Holy Communion in different ways.

Eucharist in the Orthodox Church

A Holy Communion Service in an Orthodox church

In the Orthodox Church, the Holy Communion service is called the Eucharist. Eucharist means thanksgiving. The priest has a central role. Most orthodox churches don't have seats so worshippers stand and move about during services. The communion service or eucharist can last up to three hours.

The church is divided in two by a screen with icons. The icons are designed to produce a sense of holiness and awe. The priest stays behind the icon screen when preparing the bread and wine. The high point of the service is the consecration of the bread and wine on the altar, using the words spoken by Jesus at the Last Supper.

Before this there are processions. The priest is accompanied by the altar boys carrying lights and banners. First the Gospels are brought in for all to see. This represents the coming of Jesus into the world. It is followed by readings and a short sermon. Then the bread and wine are carried in. This represents the death and burial of Jesus.

Worshippers taking communion come forward and receive communion from the priest. This is given in the form of the bread dipped in wine and served to the worshipper on a spoon.

All during the service there is singing and spoken prayers with responses. The creed and the Lord's Prayer are recited. There is usually incense and the kissing of icons and crosses.

The Breaking of Bread

In some Christian churches, communion is a very simple thing. Daniel explains what he likes about his church's approach. Daniel is fourteen and goes to the Church of God Meeting House.

> Of course it's up to other Christians how they do communion, but I like ours. There's nothing formal or stuffy about it. We just all sit together and pass round bread and wine. Whoever is leading the worship that day might say a few words, but our thoughts are our own. Anyone can stand up and speak or offer a prayer – even me. We might sing a song, usually a straightforward chorus with simple words and a bright tune. Although we remember the suffering and death of Jesus, we concentrate on the joy that he still lives with us. We break bread together every Sunday. It's a happy time.

Daniel

Communion wine and bread (in the form of wafers)

FINDING OUT

1. How and why is an Orthodox Church divided into two main parts?

2. Describe what happens to the bread and wine. What do they represent?

3. What is a procession? What is a gospel? What does the procession involving the 'gospels' represent?

4. Services in the Orthodox Church are very colourful with sounds, smells and images. Show how worshippers' five senses are all engaged during the communion service. In what way do you think this helps Orthodox Christians to worship?

5. Describe the communion ceremony which Daniel follows. What does Daniel's church remember during this ceremony? What does it concentrate on? How often does Daniel's church have communion?

6. What would you say were the main differences between communion in the Orthodox Church and in the Church of God Meeting House? Show the differences in a table such as the one below.

Orthodox Church	Church of God Meeting House
Communion known as Eucharist	Communion called breaking of bread

7. Invite a Church of Scotland Minister and a Roman Catholic Priest to describe communion in their church.

Thinking it over

❶ Communion in an Orthodox Church can last three hours. What might be the advantages and disadvantages of this?

❷ Why might some Christians prefer an Orthodox communion service and why might some Christians prefer the breaking of bread communion service?

❸ Communion is so important it should be held at least once a week.

Communion is so important it should be only held occasionally such as about once every three months.

Whose view do you agree with? Why?

stimulus
3 # The Meaning of Holy Communion

Below, different Christians explain what Communion means to them.

Sharing
When I take communion I do so with others. We help each other be strong in the face of life's difficulties. We drink from a common cup to show that we are a family. We offer the Sign of Peace to show that we will look out for each other. We have a meal at the end of communion which anyone can come to – you don't have to pay for it. This is one way of turning communion into what it should be – a way of sharing what God has given us. In Jesus' day, bread and wine was the basic foodstuff of life. For me as a Christian, Jesus gives meaning to my life – he is my daily bread. I want to share that with others.

John

Remembering
When I take communion I am thinking about the life of Jesus. I'm thinking how much God cares for us that he sacrificed his only son to save us from ourselves. I'm thinking of Jesus too, who suffered so horribly. I saw that film *The Passion of the Christ* recently and it really hit home just how terrible the whole crucifixion was. I remember that Jesus went through that for me – even though he could have chosen not to bother. If he can put up with all of that for me, then I can put up with a wee bit of discomfort to help others. I stand in the cold every Saturday night helping the homeless to a hot meal. It's not much, but Jesus gave himself for me, so I have to do something in return.

Susan

Celebrating
I don't think of the Eucharist as a sombre and sad occasion. It is a reminder to me that Jesus kept his promise. He promised to rise from the dead and he did. He promised to be with us always and he is. The Eucharist is a celebration – it is our way of remembering every week that Jesus is alive and is a constant presence in our lives. Whatever I do, Jesus is with me. Now that means when things are bad I know that he'll be there for me. It also means that when I'm tempted to do things which aren't so good I'll think twice about it! Jesus said we were to remember him in the breaking of bread. I don't think he meant we should do that with long faces but with joy and smiles. He's still here after all.

Angela

Thanking
Jesus told us that we should do like he did in the Last Supper. So I do what he says. This is my way, well one of them anyway, of thanking him for his life. In my life there are so many things I'm grateful for. I feel that I owe God for all of these things. Standing up for him at communion is one way of showing that I'm grateful – it's a small sacrifice to make.

Peter

Preserving
Christians have celebrated the Eucharist since Jesus died and rose again. It's important to keep these traditions alive. If we keep these practices going then it helps the faith to survive into the future. I sacrifice my time now for the future of the faith.

Brian

FINDING OUT

❶ For John the main point of communion is about sharing. Explain how and why this is.

❷ What does Susan remember when taking communion?

❸ What does Susan do every Saturday night? Why?

❹ Explain why Angela believes communion is a celebration and an occasion for joy rather than sadness.

❺ What is Peter saying thank you for at communion? What kind of things might Peter grateful for?

❻ Why does Brian celebrate communion?

❼ Write a paragraph explaining, in your own words, the meaning of communion for Christians.

MAKING CONNECTIONS

❶ Think over your life so far. Which events stand out in your memory? Why are they important?

❷ People often like to remember loved ones who have died. How do they usually do this?

❸ Design an illustrated poster to include:
- Things I share.
- Things I remember.
- Things I celebrate.
- Things I am grateful for.
- Traditions which should be kept alive.

❹ Think about celebrations you know or take part in – which ones are happy and which are sad? How are they celebrated?

❺ What do you have to share with others? What would you like others to share with you?

❻ On what occasions do you sit down to share a meal with friends or family? Put together a menu for a meal to share with a few of your friends.

stimulus
4　*Making a sacrifice*

Jesus said 'The greatest love a person can have for his friends is to give his life for them' (John 15:13)

In Canterbury Cathedral is a martyrs' chapel dedicated to Christians who have given their life for others in the twentieth century.

Canterbury Cathedral

Dietrich Bonhoeffer 1906–45	Theologian	Hanged for plotting against Hitler.
Jonathan Daniels 1939–1965	Theological student	Shot on a civil rights campaign in USA.
Martin Luther King 1929–1968	Baptist Minister	Assassinated on a civil rights campaign.
Maximilian Kolbe 1894–1941	Priest	Died in Auschwitz, replacing another prisoner condemned to death.
Janani Luwum 1927–1977	Archbishop	Murdered in Uganda upholding human rights.
Oscar Romero 1917–1980	Archbishop	Murdered for speaking up for human rights.
Maria Skobtsova 1891–1945	Nun	Died in gas chamber for helping Jews.

Oscar Romero

Oscar Romero was a Roman Catholic Archbishop in the South American country of El Salvador. He spoke out against the brutal ways in which the Government of El Salvador treated the poor. At first he didn't want to speak out because he thought that Christians should not get involved in politics. But when some of his priests who did speak out were killed, he changed his mind. In March 1980 he was celebrating the Eucharist. Soldiers kicked the doors of the church open and raised their guns. Romero was killed.

Oscar Romero believed that a Christian had to make sacrifices. He believed that Christians should not just teach God's message to the poor, but live alongside them and work with them. In speaking his mind for the poor he ended up sacrificing his life. Some think that his message of sacrifice was all the more powerful because he died celebrating Jesus' sacrifice on the cross. The government of El Salvador was replaced in 1991 with a new democratic government.

> May Christ's sacrifice give us the courage to offer our own bodies for Justice and Peace.

These are said to be the last words spoken by Oscar Romero.

1 Who was Oscar Romero? Where did he live and what was his job?

2 What two things did he think Christians should do?

3 Why did he change his mind about speaking out against the Government?

4 How was he killed?

5 Look at the last words of Romero. Explain what they mean.

6 Design an information poster on the beliefs and work of Oscar Romero.

7 What is a martyr?

8 Look at the list of martyrs remembered in Canterbury Cathedral. Produce a time line according to the date each died.

9 For each, match the reason for their death to one of the categories below:

Fighting evil   Upholding human rights
        Caring for others

10 Produce a class booklet headed 'Christian Martyrs'. Work in small groups and investigate one of the martyrs remembered in Canterbury Cathedral.

11 In what way have all these people followed the example of Jesus?

MAKING CONNECTIONS

1 When did you last complain about something you believed to be wrong? What was it? Why did you do it? Was it for yourself or on behalf of someone else?

2 Have you ever made a sacrifice for someone – a member of your family or a friend? Describe the circumstances? What effect did it have on them? How did you feel afterwards?

Thinking it over

1 'You should always put others first.' Do you agree or disagree? Are there times when you should put yourself first?

2 In what ways does making sacrifices for others make you a better person? What does it mean to be a better person?

3 Do you think people should stand up for what's right even if it puts them in danger? Do you think Oscar Romero was right to speak out against the Government? Explain your answer.

4 What things, if any, do you think are worth dying for?

5 Do you agree with the saying of Jesus about the greatest love a person can show is to die for his friends? Why/why not?

6 'Religious people have no business meddling in politics.' Do you agree or disagree? Give reasons for your answer?

7 Some people think Oscar Romero was a saint. What might make them think this? What do you think?

Creation

This unit explores what Christians believe about creation. It looks at the stories of creation found in the first book of the Bible, the Book of Genesis, and explores Christian views about the origins of the universe and human life. It also explores Christian attitudes to the environment. A key question in this unit is – was the universe created for a purpose or is it the result of natural forces?

IN THIS SECTION YOU WILL BE ASKED TO THINK ABOUT ...

✓ Creation

✓ Truth

✓ The existence of God

✓ Ecology and stewardship

stimulus 1 *The story of creation*

In the beginning, when God created the universe, the earth was formless and desolate. The raging ocean that covered everything was engulfed in total darkness, and the power of God was moving over the water.

Then God commanded, 'Let there be light', and light appeared. God was pleased with what he saw. Then he separated the light from the darkness, and he named the light 'day' and the darkness 'night'. Evening passed and morning came – that was the first day.

Then God commanded, 'Let there be a dome to divide the water and to keep it in two separate places', and it was done. So God made a dome, and it separated the water under it from the water above it. He named the dome 'sky'. Evening passed and morning came – that was the second day.

Then God commanded, 'Let the water below the sky come together in one place, so that the land will appear', and it was done. He named the land 'earth', and the water which had come together he named 'sea'. And God was pleased with what he saw. Then he commanded, 'Let the earth produce all kinds of plants, those that bear grain and those that bear fruit', and it was done. So the earth produced all kinds of plants and God was pleased with what he saw. Evening passed and morning came – that was the third day.

Then God commanded, 'Let lights appear in the sky to separate day from night and to show the time when days, years and religious festivals begin; they will shine in the sky to give light to the earth', and it was done. So

God made the two larger lights the sun to rule over the day and the moon to rule over the night; he also made the stars. He placed the lights in the sky to shine on the earth, to rule over the day and the night, and to separate light from darkness. And God was pleased with what he saw. Evening passed and morning came – that was the fourth day.

Then God commanded, 'Let the water be filled with many kinds of living beings, and let the air be filled with birds.' So God created the great sea-monsters, all kinds of creatures that live in the water, and all kinds of birds. And God was pleased with what he saw. He blessed them all and told the creatures that live in the water to reproduce, and to fill the sea, and he told the birds to increase in number. Evening passed and morning came – that was the fifth day.

Then God commanded, 'Let the earth produce all kinds of animal life: domestic and wild, large and small', and it was done. So God made them all and he was pleased with what he saw. Then God said, 'And now we will make human beings; they will be like us and resemble us. They will have power over the fish, the birds and all animals, domestic and wild, large and small.' So God created human beings, making them to be like himself. He created them male and female, blessed them, and said, 'Have many

children, so that your descendants will live all over the earth and bring it under their control. I am putting you in charge of the fish, the birds and all the wild animals. I have provided all kinds of grain and all kinds of fruit for you to eat; but for all the wild animals and for all the birds I have provided grass and leafy plants for food', and it was done. God looked at everything he had made, and he was very pleased. Evening passed and morning came – that was the sixth day.

And so the whole universe was completed. By the seventh day God finished what he had been doing and stopped working. He blessed the seventh day and set it apart as a special day, because by that day he had completed his creation and stopped working. And that is how the universe was created. (Genesis, 1–2,4)

❶ Put the parts of the biblical creation story into the right order. Match each part to a day. Use the parts to produce a visual picture of the biblical creation story.
   • God made flowers and trees.
   • There was nothing, but God's spirit was there.
   • God said 'let there be light'.
   • God separated the land from the sea.
   • God separated earth from the heavens.
   • God separated day from night.
   • God finished the job and had a day of rest.
   • God made the the sun and moon.
   • God made man.
   • God made the birds of the air and life in the oceans.

❷ Look at the first paragraph of the creation story. What words suggest that at the beginning everything was chaos?

❸ In this account, a number of phrases are repeated several times. They include 'Then God commanded'; 'And it was done'; ' God was (very) pleased'. Count the number of times these phrases are in the account. Why do you think they occur so often?

❹ In this account what special jobs are humans given regarding the created world?

❺ Read Genesis, 2:4–25 for another biblical account of creation. Work in pairs and note down how the accounts are similar and how they are different.

MAKING CONNECTIONS

❶ Have you ever created something like an artefact or a piece of music or a poem or a painting which pleased you? What was it? Why did it please you?

❷ When something is described as 'awesome' what is meant? Working as part of a group, prepare a visual presentation for the class on the theme 'What we find awesome about the world'.

❸ Think of a time in your life when you experienced something like awe or wonder. Describe the occasion in a piece of personal writing explaining the effect it had on you and why it was unforgettable.

❹ What is meant by the word 'vast'? Can you remember a time when you said, 'This is vast'? When was it? Can you describe your feelings?

Thinking it over

❶ Which do you think is more awesome, the vastness of natural places such as mountains and canyons or human constructions such as buildings or cruise liners? What makes you say that?

❷ Do you think the vastness of the universe makes human life on earth more or less important? Why/why not? What difference would it make if the universe was much smaller?

❸ Do you think the vastness of the universe makes the existence of God more or less likely? Why/why not?

❹ Are humans more important than the rest of creation? Give reasons for your opinion.

stimulus 2 — Questions about the story

Connor is in first year at Libermount High School. He comes from a Christian family. The more he learns in school, the more he wonders about the creation story. At home, he asks his Dad a few questions.

Connor: Dad, how come God made everything in six days?

Dad: Why not? He's God after all, and that means he's as powerful as can be.

Connor: Yeah… but Dad… the Bible story's a bit unlikely isn't it.

Dad: Well, it's unlikely that an elephant is about to walk in our front door...

Connor: Huh?

Dad: Just because it *seems* unlikely doesn't mean it *is*. There just might be an escaped elephant running around outside or a TV surprise show about to spring a big joke on me…

Connor: Oh for goodness sake Dad. But there was no one there to see the creation.

Dad: God was, and he let us know about it in the Bible. And if only God was there, then there wasn't anyone else around to prove him wrong was there?

Connor: But Dad, it just all seems like some kind of fairy story. One of my teachers said it was just a myth.

Dad: Is the story of the tortoise and the hare a true story?

Connor: Come on….

Dad: No, it's a story with a message. You don't hear anyone complaining about that being a terrible lie we tell our kids. It's just a helpful way of explaining some important ideas. Maybe the Creation story is the same. It says that God made everything.

Connor: But Dad, it's so weird…

Dad: Weird schmeird. OK Connor, imagine God explained exactly how he created the universe, all maths symbols, physics laws and Einstein stuff, do you think you'd understand?

Connor: Probably not, I can hardly cope with my maths teacher's explanations of arithmetic.

Dad: And what if I started to explain to you how to produce complex polymers like I do at work?

Connor: OK Dad, enough, enough.

Dad: Exactly. You don't need to know that and you probably wouldn't understand it even if I made it completely idiot-proof.

Connor: But could you do that Dad?

Dad: Yeah, I might be able to… by telling you a simple story about Mr and Mrs Polymer and their strung out family all lined up in a row…

Connor: Fair enough. So is that the point of the Bible story?

Dad: Well, I think the Bible story helps me get a general idea of something incredibly complicated. It's there to tell us that God created everything – not how he did it, just that he did it. It doesn't even look like a scientific account of how the universe might have come about. It tells us that God made the world, that he made people to be like himself and that people themselves are responsible for what happens to their world.

Christians believe God created everything in six days

① Look up a dictionary to find out different meanings of the word 'myth'. Which meaning do you think best applies to the story of creation in Stimulus 1? What makes you say that?

② Carry out some research into 'creation myths' from around the world, for example, from North America and Africa. How are these similar to or different from the story of creation in Genesis?

③ What does Connor's dad say are the main messages of the Genesis story of creation?

④ Do you think Connor's dad believes that the world was created in six days? What makes you think that? What does he believe?

⑤ a) What elements of the natural world might a Christian cite as 'evidence' that the world was created by God?

b) What is it about these particular elements that convince Christians God must have created the world?

Thinking it over

① Read the following statements. Which do you agree or disagree with? Copy out the table and write agree or disagree in the spaces provided. Give reasons for your decision or include some form of evidence to support it.

Statement	Agree/Disagree
The biblical story of Creation is a way of communicating an important message.	
The biblical creation story seems like a kind of fairy story.	
God made everything in six days.	
You can't say something is untrue simply because it sounds weird.	
The Genesis story doesn't look like a scientific account of how the universe came about.	
You don't need to know how the universe was made to enjoy it.	

② When we say something is true or not true what do we mean? What makes something true? In what way can a story be true?

③ Do you think people sometimes refuse to believe things simply because they appear unlikely? Does this make sense?

④ Virtually all religions and cultures have a story about the beginning of the world. Why do you think this is?

The origin of the universe

What do we know about the origin of the universe?

It all came from the Big Bang some fifteen or twenty thousand million years ago. Initially, everything was concentrated into a very, very dense spot (for want of a better word) and this exploded. And out of that explosion came everything: all space, all time, all matter, all energy. And since then it has been gradually expanding and cooling. Initially it was a great ball of energy, but with time that turned into matter. Dust and gases were pulled together by gravity and other powerful forces to form stars and planets like Earth.

What happened after that?

Chemicals started to go through weird and wonderful changes becoming less like chemicals and more like living things. Simple living organisms became more specialised and over millions of years evolved into all kinds of plants and animals. Living things became suited to where and when they lived. Things appeared, became extinct in the struggle for survival and then were replaced – all as a result of natural selection.

Two Christian views about the Big Bang theory

I believe in the Big Bang theory and the creation story. The evidence for the Big Bang theory is so powerful it has to be true. But that doesn't push God out of the picture. I think only God could have done something like that, and I don't think science can ever prove or disprove that God did or didn't start everything off. The Bible story makes it clear that it was God who started the world. The science of the Big Bang gives me a clue about how God did it, but not why he did it. Finding out the science behind the creation doesn't help me to know how I should live my life or how I should treat things. It doesn't give my life any more purpose. In fact, the more science tells me about how the Universe began or how life on Earth developed, the more incredible it makes the creator seem to me.

Jessica

The first words of the Bible are 'In the beginning God created the Heavens and the Earth'. Now here's the thing. If I don't believe the first words of this book, what would be the point of reading on any further? Why would God's word say he did something he didn't do? It just doesn't make sense. I'm not stupid, I know about the Big Bang theory – but it is only a theory. My life is based on faith in God, not scientific proof. The Bible works for me in every other way. Why shouldn't this be right too? God said it; I believe it. That's what faith is all about.

Robin

① Using the scientific explanation above and your own knowledge of the Big Bang theory, explain in your own words the scientific explanation of how the world came into being and plant and animal life began.

② What does Jessica think of the Big Bang theory?

③ In what way does the Big Bang theory not answer all of Jessica's questions?

④ Why does Robin not accept the Big Bang theory?

Thinking it over

① Did the universe begin itself or did something make it happen? What do you think?

② Why do you think some scientists who believe in the Big Bang are Christians?

③ Look again at Jessica's and Robin's views. For each say why you agree or disagree with their view.

④ Read the two statements below:

'Science and religion can never agree. Science says one thing about the beginning of the world; religion another.'

'Science answers questions about how the world started; religion answers questions about why the world started. They are not in disagreement – they are looking at things in different ways.'

Which statement comes nearer to your own views? Why? Do you agree that science and religion are answering different questions?

4 Trying to prove the existence of God

Many Christians believe that the fact the universe exists is proof that there is a God. There are two famous arguments which aim to show this proof.

The First Cause Argument

1 Everything which exists must have a cause.
2 The universe exists.
3 So the universe must have a cause.
4 Things can't go backwards forever, being caused by one thing after another.
5 So there had to be a first cause.
6 The only thing powerful enough to be a first cause is God.
7 So …God must exist.

The Argument from Design

1 Everything in the Universe is just right for its job.
2 It looks like it has been designed that way.
3 If something is designed it can't have happened by chance.
4 So there must have been a designer which designed the universe and everything in the universe.
5 The only thing which could design everything in the universe is God.
6 So God must exist.

A man called William Paley tried to explain the argument from design. He said if you were out having a walk and came across a stone, you would probably think (if you thought about it at all) this stone has always been here. But if you came across a watch, you would ask where it had come from. You might pick it up and have a look at it and see its complex mechanism. You would conclude that the watch did not come about by chance. It must have been designed. So with the universe. It is a complex mechanism. Just like a watch it must have had a designer. Only intelligence could have produced the universe. This designer, this intelligence, is God.

Thinking it over

1 Have a debate in class based on the First Cause Argument. Here are some statements to help your discussion:
- Why does everything have to have a cause?
- If everything has to have a cause, why does God not need to have a cause?
- Why can't the universe just have always existed?
- Even if there was a first cause how do we know it was the God of Christianity?
- How do we know that God didn't cause the universe and then disappear?
- If there was no space and time, where and when did God cause the universe?

2 Look at these four opinions about the Argument from Design:

> The universe is so complex and beautiful it must have had a designer – God.

> If God designed the universe he should have done a better job.

> There's no God; the universe came about just by chance.

> There's a plan and a purpose for the universe and everything in the universe.

Which view is nearest your own? Give reasons for your answer.

3 Which Argument do you think is better – the Argument from Design or the First Cause Argument? Give reasons for your view.

4 Some Christians say it is impossible to prove that God does or does not exist. What do you think?

5 Can you believe in something even if there is no proof?

stimulus 5 Christians and the environment

Christians believe that humans are stewards of God's creation. Stewards look after things which belong to others, preserving and protecting them from harm. A good steward takes what he needs from the Earth and no more. The Bible teaches that the Earth and everything in it belongs to God. He allows humans to live on it and provides everything that they need to enjoy a happy life. It wouldn't make any sense to do it harm.

> 'I am putting you (humans) in charge of the fish, the birds, and all the wild animals.' (Genesis, 1:28)

Christian Ecology Link (CEL) is an organisation which tries to get Christians to take environmental issues seriously and put their faith into action on the environment. They aim to:

- Offer insights into ecology and the environment to Christian people and churches.
- Offer Christian insights into the Green movement.

They say: 'We are responsible for our impact on God's creation as a whole. We help members to understand their relationship to the environment and so help others in their churches to do the same. This will encourage people in churches to think seriously about environmental issues.'
(www.christian-ecology.org.uk)

> I believe I have a responsibility to look after the planet on which I live because this is a way of thanking God for the gift of the world.
> (Christian environmental worker)

FINDING OUT

❶ What do Christians mean when they say, 'humans are stewards of God's creation'?

❷ Have humans acted as good stewards of the created world? Give evidence to back up your answer and make up a collage of images to illustrate your answer.

❸ What is Christian Ecology Link and what does it aim to do?

❹ What reason does the Christian environmental worker give for looking after the planet?

❺ What other reasons are there for looking after the planet?

MAKING CONNECTIONS

❶ Think about the phrase 'I am putting you in charge of...' What does it mean? Have you ever been put in charge of something? What was it like? What responsibilities did you have?

❷ The Bible says humans are in charge of the created world. What do you do that harms the world?

❸ Do you do enough to protect the environment? What more could you do? Make yourself a 'New Year resolution list' (you could start putting it into action today) about things you are going to do to help look after the environment. Collect all the answers of what you can do and display them in the classroom.

❹ Design a poster which encourages people to care for the environment. Make sure that the poster explains what they could do and why they should do it.

You may find some of the following websites helpful
- www.christian-ecology.org.uk
- www.reep.org.uk
- www.srtp.org.uk/srtpage3.shtml
- www.jri.org.uk/

Easter

For many Christians Easter is the most important festival. This unit looks at the events leading up to Easter and explores the beliefs, practices and meaning of the festival of Easter. It considers the evidence concerning Christian belief in Jesus' resurrection and focuses on Easter celebrations within the Christian Orthodox tradition.

IN THIS SECTION YOU WILL BE ASKED TO THINK ABOUT ...

✓ Guilt and shame

✓ Hope

✓ Mystery

✓ Resurrection

Personal Search

stimulus 1 *The death of Jesus*

Well it's all over. What a time it has been over the last twenty-four hours or so. There we were Thursday night all us friends of Jesus having the Passover meal together, when Jesus dropped a bombshell. One of us would betray him he said. We couldn't understand it. But later that night we went out to the Garden of Gethsemane and Jesus asked us to

watch out for him while he prayed, but we fell asleep. And then it happened. It was Judas. He came with a band of armed men sent by the Jewish leaders, and he kissed Jesus on the cheek – a sign that Jesus was the one the armed men wanted and Jesus was led away. I heard later that he had done it for thirty pieces of silver. We all ran away, but later followed from a safe distance. In fact Peter was accused of being a friend and follower of Jesus, but he was so scared he denied it. I don't blame him. I think I would have done the same. Afterwards I felt so guilty and ashamed that we had let Jesus down. We had deserted him in his hour of need.

Jesus was taken before the Jewish leaders to be tried and later they sent him to the Roman Governor, Pontius Pilate, because he was the only one who had the power to have Jesus sentenced to death. Pilate offered to release Jesus, as it was a custom at festival time for a prisoner to be released. But the crowd roared that they wanted a terrorist called Barabbas released and not Jesus. So Pilate gave in. He had Jesus beaten up and humiliated and then handed him over to be crucified. I watched as Jesus was forced to carry his cross to Golgotha, the place of crucifixion. It was awful. I won't go into the details of the crucifixion but nobody should have to die in that way. After Jesus' death, his body was taken down and placed in a tomb of a man called Joseph of Arimathea.

So that's it. A great man. A good man. A great teacher. A man I had followed for three years. A man I thought would be a great leader. But now he's dead. I'll never forget him but that's the end. It's all over.

❶ Use the above account to explain how Judas and Peter let Jesus down.

❷ Explain why this imaginary disciple felt guilty and ashamed.

❸ Read the account of the events of Jesus' death from Mark's Gospel.

The betrayal and arrest	Mark, 14:10–11 and Mark, 14:43–51
The trial before the Jewish leaders	Mark, 14:53–65
Peter denies Jesus	Mark, 14:27–31 and Mark, 14:66–72
The trial before Pontius Pilate	Mark, 15:1–15
The beating up of Jesus	Mark, 15:16–20
The crucifixion	Mark, 15:21–32
The death of Jesus	Mark, 15:33–41
The burial	Mark, 15:42–47

❹ Work in groups. Each group should focus on one of the sections of the story to produce a written and visual presentation of it. Use the work of each group to present a wall display.

MAKING CONNECTIONS

❶ The disciples let Jesus down. Describe a time you let someone down. Why were you unhappy about having done it? What would you wish to happen if you could go back and start again?

❷ Describe a time when you felt ashamed or guilty. Was this for something you did or for something you failed to do? Do you feel more guilty for doing something you shouldn't do or for not doing something you should? Why do you think this is?

❸ What do you do when you feel guilty? Does it help to talk to someone? Would the person that you talk to depend on what you were feeling guilty about?

❹ In groups, discuss ideas for a short story entitled 'I felt really guilty'. Write your own story based on the ideas you discussed.

Thinking it over

❶ Who do you think was to blame for the death of Jesus? Choose one of the following and give reasons for your answer. Compare your answers with the rest of the class.

Judas   Peter   Jewish Leaders   Pontius Pilate

Ordinary Jews   Jesus   God

❷ A Roman army officer who watched Jesus die on the cross said, 'This man (Jesus) was really the Son of God.' (Mark, 15:39) Discuss in class what you think this means and why the Roman army officer said it.

2

Was death the end? Easter Sunday

'Don't be alarmed', he said. 'I know you are looking for Jesus of Nazareth who was crucified. He is not here – he has been raised! Look, here is the place where they put him. Now go and give this message to his disciples, including Peter: He is going to Galilee ahead of you; there you will see him, just as he told you.' So they went out and ran from the tomb, distressed and terrified. They said nothing to anyone, because they were afraid. (Mark, 16:1–8)

After the Sabbath was over, Mary Magdalene, Mary the mother of James, and Salome bought spices to go and anoint the body of Jesus. Very early on Sunday morning, at sunrise, they went to the tomb. On the way they said to one another, 'Who will roll away the stone for us from the entrance to the tomb?' Then they looked up and saw that the stone had already been rolled back. So they entered the tomb, where they saw a young man sitting on the right, wearing a white robe – and they were alarmed.

❶ According to the gospel writer, Mark, why did Mary Magdalene, Mary the mother of James, and Salome go to the tomb early on the Sunday morning?

❷ What did they find when they got there?

❸ What did the young man in the white robe tell them?

❹ How did the women react to this news? Why do you think they reacted in this way?

❺ Design a newspaper front page about the tomb being found empty.

6 Find out what appearances of the 'resurrected' Jesus are recorded in the New Testament. Read for example Paul's first letter to the Corinthians, 15:3–8.

7 The Resurrection is often described as a mystery. What is a mystery? Why do you think the Resurrection is described as mysterious?

3 The meaning of the Resurrection

Two Christians were asked what Easter and the Resurrection of Jesus means to them.

Joe: As a Christian, it matters to me that the Resurrection really happened and Jesus physically rose from the dead. Of course I don't have proof, but then proof isn't everything.

Some say Jesus didn't really die on the cross but I think that Jesus must have died on the cross. The Romans were ruthless but very efficient. When a soldier was given a job to do, he would have made sure it was done properly. No, I don't think there's really any doubt that Jesus died.

Others argue Jesus' body was stolen! But the Roman guards were too good to have let that happen. It wouldn't have been easy to steal a body anyway, and besides, Jewish people had very strict rules about touching the dead. Anyway, the followers were in hiding. They weren't going to break cover to pull a stunt like that I don't think.

Some even argue that the disciples made up the story of the Resurrection. I don't think so! When Jesus was killed these men were terrified as the story of Peter shows. The man they loved had died, just like a common criminal. As his followers they were in great danger. If they didn't keep out of sight they might end up being executed too. So they hid away in the shadows. Then, for some reason, they started to proclaim that Jesus has risen from the dead. The most frightened men in the Roman Empire turned into either the craziest, or the bravest men in the Empire… or just completely convinced that their master was back from the grave.

Perhaps. Some argue the disciples imagined it all and they experienced some kind of hallucination. But that's no answer either. There were far too many encounters with the risen Jesus for that. He appeared to individuals, to the apostles and to large numbers of his followers. They couldn't all have imagined it.

They all lived their lives clinging to the belief that they had seen Jesus resurrected, and succeeded in convincing thousands of others who hadn't seen him. Only things which have the ring of truth about them can grow and stand the test of time. Two thousand and more years later millions of people still follow him. That's enough proof as far as I'm concerned.

So for me the Resurrection is a real historical event. In some way Jesus' body literally emerged from the grave and it shows that God has power over death and that He has saved people from sin if they follow him and put their trust in him.

Brenda: Well I differ a bit from Joe. For me, like Joe, the Resurrection of Jesus is really important and a great mystery which I'll never fully understand. However, I believe that the Resurrection is not about a dead body coming back to life, but it is more of a spiritual sign showing that although wicked men killed Jesus, they could not kill what he stood for. For me the resurrection is a sign that the goodness and love which Jesus showed in his life cannot be silenced. Jesus showed that love is stronger than hate; forgiveness better than revenge. Good Friday was a day of sadness but Easter is a day of joy. Good Friday was a day of darkness, but Easter is a day of light. For me Easter means that there is always hope, even in times of despair and defeat.

Let me give an example of what I mean. Several years ago in Northern Ireland there was a bomb in a town called Enniskillen which killed many people. A man called Gordon Wilson was with his daughter that day, and she died from the bomb but he survived. This was a dark, sad day. The events could have made Gordon Wilson a bitter person, but he refused to let it do so. His Christian faith was that love could overcome evil and so for the rest of his life he worked for peace and reconciliation in Northern Ireland. He followed the example of Jesus believing that love was the best way and even death and evil acts cannot destroy love.

So for me the resurrection means that in the end despair and evil cannot win and love and goodness will be victorious.

FINDING OUT

❶ Look at the following statements.
- I believe Jesus rose from the dead and this shows there is life after death.
- I believe that the Resurrection is a sign that love conquers evil.

Which statement is nearer Joe's view and which is nearer Brenda's view?

❷ Joe discusses four arguments often used to disprove the Resurrection – what are they? For each argument explain why Joe finds it unconvincing.

❸ Joe says that the Resurrection shows God, through Jesus, has saved people from sin if they follow him. Discuss in class what Joe means by this.

❹ Brenda explains her beliefs by using a series of contrasts such as Good Friday – despair; Easter – hope. What other contrasts does she use?

❺ Design a contrast poster. On one side could be the misery of Good Friday (drawings of nails, a dice, crucifix, the use of dark colours, sad words etc.) and on the other side the joy of Easter (joyful words, Easter symbols etc.).

❻ Discuss how Brenda uses the example of Gordon Wilson to explain her understanding of Easter.

❼ Invite a Christian Minister to your class to explain why Easter is important. Before the visit write down two questions you would like to ask.

Thinking it over

❶ Do you agree with Joe that there is enough evidence to prove that Jesus physically rose from the dead? In groups discuss the arguments he introduces and the reasons he gives for not accepting them. Try to come to your own conclusion.

❷ Some Christians believe it is impossible to prove the Resurrection – it has to be accepted on faith. What do you think they mean by this? Is there anything you believe that cannot be proved?

❸ Some Christians like Joe believe that because Jesus was raised from the dead everyone will be resurrected. What do you think survives after death, if anything? Four possibilities are set out below. Choose *one* and give reasons for your decision.
   a) Both the soul or spirit of the person and the body survive in some form – as in resurrection.
   b) The soul, which then enters a new body – as in reincarnation.
   c) The soul alone – as in some kind of ghostly existence.
   d) Nothing survives – as atheists believe.

❹ Which is more difficult to believe – that Jesus physically rose from the dead or that love will always overcome evil?

❺ Do you believe that some day we will have an answer for everything or are there some things, such as the Resurrection, that will always remain a mystery?

stimulus 4 *An Easter Hymn*

Christ the Lord, is risen today, Alleluia!
Sons of men and angels say, Alleluia!
Raise your joys and triumphs high, Alleluia!
Sing, ye heavens, and earth reply, Alleluia!

Love's redeeming work is done, Alleluia!
Fought the fight, the battle won, Alleluia!
Lo! The Sun's eclipse is over, Alleluia!
Lo! He sets in blood no more, Alleluia!

Vain the stone, the watch, the seal, Alleluia!
Christ hath burst the gates of hell, Alleluia!
Death in vain forbids His rise, Alleluia!
Christ hath opened Paradise, Alleluia!

Lives again our glorious King, Alleluia!
Where, O death, is now thy sting? Alleluia!
Once He died our souls to save, Alleluia!
Where thy victory, O Grave Alleluia!

Soar we now where Christ has led, Alleluia!
Following our exalted Head, Alleluia!
Made like Him, like Him we rise, Alleluia!
Ours the cross, the grave, the skies, Alleluia!

Hail, the Lord of earth and heaven, Alleluia!
Praise to Thee by both be given, Alleluia!
Thee we greet triumphant now, Alleluia!
Hail the resurrection day, Alleluia!

Charles Wesley 1739

FINDING OUT

❶ If possible, listen to a sung version of this hymn. How would you describe the tune?

❷ Reading through the hymn, does it strike you as a happy hymn or a sad one? Give one piece of evidence for your choice

❸ Find out what the word 'Alleluia' means. Why is it at the end of every line?

❹ Which lines show the belief that Jesus (Christ) has conquered death and that death has no power.

❺ Which lines suggest the belief that Christians will follow Christ into heaven?

❻ Verse two has the line 'fought the fight, the battle won'. What is the battle Christians believe has been fought?

❼ This is a difficult hymn. In groups write a simpler hymn to celebrate Easter. It should be a happy, joyous hymn.

Easter in the Orthodox Church

Hello, my name is Olivia Kantazis and I'm twelve years old. Lots of things have happened over the past month to prepare for our biggest celebration of the year. It's been really serious. But now it's nearly Easter Sunday and things are getting a lot more fun. If we'd been back home in Greece, then the whole village would have been involved. You'd smell roasting goat all over the place and whenever you walked down a street you'd be offered a bit of goat to eat. Families would get together and get ready for the Easter Sunday celebrations.

It's not the same in Britain, but at least all the Greeks living here get together in the Church to get the party going! It's really late now, nearly midnight, and I'm already a bit tired, but the Church is full, and we're standing around waiting. The Church is really dark and people are stony silent. It's like you're holding your breath.

It's not sad like a couple of days ago though. On Friday we were in here and there was a cloth carried around with an icon of Jesus dead on it. The priests were all dressed in black and very miserable – even Father Alex who's usually a funny guy. We said sad prayers and kissed the icon – honestly, it was just like a funeral. But tonight people aren't so down. The altar doors are closed, and we know that on the other side are the priests ready to come through at midnight. We've all got a candle, but it isn't lit yet.

At midnight the bells ring out and they shatter the silence. The doors of the altar burst open and the priests arrive. They're dressed in white with bright colours too. Each holds a candle. Father Alex, now with his usual beaming smile, chants very loudly; 'Christ is risen!' The whole place, me included, replies, 'He is risen indeed!'

The Priests come round and light each of our candles. Now the whole place is really bright and colourful and cheerful. The bells keep ringing. People shake hands and sometimes cuddle each other. When I was in Greece, people outside would be setting off fireworks and sometimes even shooting guns in the air! But here, there's enough noise inside to make up for not having that!

This is great fun. Tomorrow will be great too when we get our red eggs at the end of the Agape service – and go home to a brilliant dinner – and maybe even a nice present!

FINDING OUT

❶ According to Olivia what is different about Easter celebrations in Greece?

❷ Describe what happened in church on Friday and what the atmosphere was like?

❸ Describe what happens when the bells ring at midnight. In what ways is the atmosphere different from the Friday service?

❹ What words are said by the priests and people? What is the atmosphere like afterwards? Why do Christians believe these words give them hope?

❺ What is Olivia looking forward to?

❻ Find out what happens at an Easter service in *either*, the Roman Catholic Church, the Church of Scotland *or* the Baptist Church.

MAKING CONNECTIONS

❶ Carry out a small survey in your class/school. Ask people how they celebrate Easter and what Easter means to them. Display your findings.

❷ Have you ever seen a festival or celebration while you were on holiday in another country? Describe what you saw. Are there any similar celebrations where you live?

❸ A key idea about the Orthodox celebrations is joy. Explain why Olivia is joyful. What makes you joyful and why?

❹ A key idea about the celebration is hope. Write down your hopes for the future and say how they might be achieved. Do you have any hopes for members of your family or your friends? What are your hopes for the world?

stimulus 6 *Easter and Non-Christian Links*

In some ways Easter is a continuation of pre-Christian religious beliefs and practices, particularly those associated with the coming of Spring, which was celebrated for the renewal of plant life and the return of warm weather
after the cold 'death' of winter. The word Easter itself probably comes from the Saxon Goddess of Spring, Eostre.

In the Mediterranean area, the god Attis was believed to have died and risen three days later.

One god, Tammuz, was worshipped during springtime. His followers ate sacred cakes with the marking of a cross on top – just like a hot cross bun.

In Saxon times, an ox was sacrificed at the Eostre feast. Ox horns were carved into ritual bread. The word bun comes from the saxon 'boun' which means 'sacred ox'.

The ancient Egyptians worshipped the sun. At springtime they celebrated its rising. They also carried out rituals involving eggs.

A hare and eggs were symbols of the Norse goddess Ostara.

Eggs were symbols of fertility and new life in pre-Christian religions.

In pre-Christian religions, the rabbit or hare was thought of as a magical creature – and of course the rabbit's foot is still a good luck symbol.

FINDING OUT

❶ What is the likely origin of the word Easter?

❷ What were the symbols of the Norse Goddess, Ostara? In which countries did the Norse Gods and Goddesses feature?

❸ What are the main symbols associated with Easter and what do they signify?

MAKING CONNECTIONS

❶ Which symbols of Easter are you familiar with from your childhood? Describe your experience of them from within your family, in school, as part of a church group or other group such as Brownies, Guides, Scouts.

❷ Design an Easter card for a friend using some of the symbols mentioned in Stimulus 6 or others that you know about. What message would you want to include inside it?

❸ Is Easter a time of special celebration for you? In what way? Or is it just another holiday period?

❹ Why is 'new life' an appropriate symbol for the Christian festival of Easter? What evidence is there of new life around Easter time?

Thinking it over

❶ Some people say Easter is just too commercialised now. What do they mean? What do you think?

❷ Do you think Christians should celebrate Easter with eggs and bunnies as these are non-Christian in origin?

❸ Many people who celebrate Easter don't understand the symbolism of things like Easter eggs. Do you think this matters?

❹ For most Christians Easter is more important than Christmas. Why do you think this is?

❺ Does Easter matter to you? Why/why not?

The Sermon on the Mount

T his unit focuses on Jesus' teaching in the Sermon on the Mount. The sermon is a collection of Jesus' teaching to his disciples.

IN THIS SECTION YOU WILL BE ASKED TO THINK ABOUT …

✓ A perfect world

✓ Happiness

✓ Revenge

✓ Non-violence

✓ Money and possessions

stimulus 1 Martha's World

You can go through all the statistics you like. I did it when I was at school. We used the Internet to find out about how many millions of people in the world don't have fresh water, or how many children die of diseases whose names I can't remember. You can look at a figure like '40 per cent of this country's population live in absolute poverty', or 'a child dies every six minutes somewhere on earth because of malnutrition'. But I'm not sure I always really took this in – I don't think people do, it's just too much, and anyway it's all so far away and there's nothing really to be done.

But now I'm here and in it, it's different. Martha is a young mum. She's one of many Africans in the same boat. She has two kids. She's got Aids. She won't live much longer. She still tries to care for her kids, but she's really weak sometimes, so the kids just end up doing their own thing. When she dies there will be no one, no one at all to look after the kids. This isn't a small village where everyone looks after everyone else – it's a city where people only look after themselves.

Callum, a Christian Aid worker
(www.globalgang.org.uk)

❶ According to Callum how do people usually react to facts and figures like those in the passage? What reasons does he give to explain this?

❷ Why is his reaction to the facts completely different now?

❸ Describe Martha's situation and explain what is her biggest concern.

❹ What do you think Martha hopes for?

❺ Why do you think Callum went to Africa? What do you think he is trying to do?

❻ What do you think Callum hopes for?

❼ What do you think Callum is trying to get across in this piece of writing? Do you think he has been successful?

❽ Find some facts and figures about poverty in Africa. Do you think it is important to be aware of the facts? Why/why not?

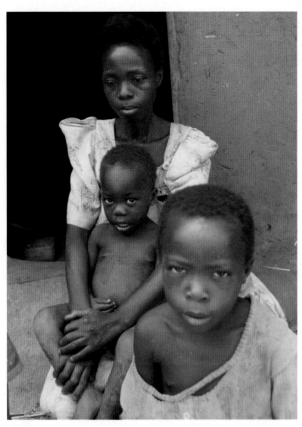

This woman is in the same situation as Martha

MAKING CONNECTIONS

❶ Think about the world you live in. Look through a typical day's newspaper. How many stories can you find that deal with the topics shown?

Politics	
Sport	
Famous celebrities	
World poverty	
Crime	
Work	

Which topic is most popular? What does this say about what people think is important?

❷ What's good about the world you live in?

❸ What's not so good about the world you live in?

❹ What in today's world concerns you and makes you worry?

❺ What do you hope for the future for the world?

 stimulus
2 *Happiness*

The passage on the following page is the opening verses of the Sermon on the Mount. It is called the Beatitudes. The word 'beatitude' means happy. The passage describes people who are favoured by God, and thus they can be described as being happy. The teaching would have surprised the listeners because it suggests that it is not the powerful and those who think they are important who are happy. Jesus believed that sometime in the future God would bring about a world where peace and justice would be the order of the day. The New Testament refers to this perfect world as the Kingdom of God or the Kingdom of Heaven and it is based upon qualities such as love, mercy, humility, forgiveness, reconciliation and peace. Its citizens would be like the people described in the Beatitudes.

Jesus addressing his disciples on the mount

Jesus saw the crowds and went up a hill, where he sat down. His disciples gathered round him, and he began to teach them:

Happy are those who know they are spiritually poor; the Kingdom of heaven belongs to them!
Happy are those who mourn; God will comfort them!
Happy are those who are humble; they will receive what God has promised!
Happy are those whose greatest desire is to do what God requires; God will satisfy them fully!
Happy are those who are merciful to others; God will be merciful to them!
Happy are the pure in heart; they will see God!
Happy are those who work for peace; God will call them his children!
Happy are those who are persecuted because they do what God requires; the Kingdom of Heaven belongs to them!

(Matthew, 5: 1–10)

FINDING OUT

❶ List the eight sorts of people in the passage who are described as being happy.

❷ For each write down what will be their reward.

❸ Discuss in class what 'spiritually poor' and 'pure in heart' means. Write down your ideas.

❹ Of all those described as being happy, which surprises you most? Why?

❺ Look again at Stimulus 1. Which category of happiness do you think Callum and Martha might belong to? Why?

MAKING CONNECTIONS

❶ What would be your recipe for a happy life?

❷ 'Happy are those who work for peace.' What would working for peace involve within your family, among your friends and in your school?

❸ What does it mean to be humble? Would you say that you were humble? Do you know anyone who is humble? What does it mean to 'make someone eat humble pie'?

❹ What does it mean to be 'merciful'? Write a short story in which someone shows mercy.

❺ Which of the statements in Matthew's passage do you think most applies to you? What makes you say that?

❻ Write some speech bubbles to complete the sentence 'For me, a perfect school would be….' Compare them with others in your class. Are there any common themes?

❼ Make a list of the things you would associate with a perfect world.

❽ Copy out the table on the following page and connect each idea for a perfect world with the person from the list below the table most likely to be associated with it:

A world where...	Person
People are free of disease.	
People have faith in something greater than themselves.	
People are free to believe whatever they want.	
People don't pick on you for no reason.	
Everyone's opinion matters whatever your age.	
All children have access to education.	
People do all they can to protect the planet.	
People get a fair day's pay for a fair day's work.	
Everyone has sufficient food and shelter.	
People are able to settle their differences peacefully.	

A Fair Trade campaigner
A teacher
A peace campaigner
A victim of bullying
Someone in prison for their beliefs

An environmental activist
Someone living in poverty
An elderly person
A Christian minister
A doctor

Thinking it over

❶ In groups discuss your vision of a perfect world. Create two lists: realistic ideas and unrealistic ideas. Is it important to have a vision of what the world could be like? How would you answer someone who said that such a vision is just an 'ideal' that will never come about?

❷ Why isn't the world perfect? Whose fault is it?

❸ Is it important to be happy? Why? Can you be happy all the time? Why/why not?

❹ Is there a difference between being happy and being content with life?

❺ Do you think people would be happy in a 'perfect' world?

❻ 'It's pointless thinking about a perfect world. It'll never happen. We can't do anything to make the world perfect.' Do you agree?

3 *Making the world a better place: turn the other cheek*

> You have heard that it was said, 'an eye for an eye, and a tooth for a tooth.' But now I tell you: do not take revenge on someone who wrongs you, if any anyone slaps you on the right cheek, let him slap your left cheek too. (Matthew, 5: 38–9)

When I was at school, I often had a hard time because I came from a strict Christian family. I'd get called 'Bible basher' and 'Jesus freak'. When I think about it, it was strange because I was much bigger than everyone in my year, and if it had ever come to a fight, I'd have beaten anyone easily. But the other kids knew I wouldn't fight so they could niggle away at me in safety. One day wee (and I mean wee) Tam in my class came up to me and punched me hard in the stomach. I think they'd dared him to do it. I got angry and grabbed him. Honestly, I'm sure wee Tam nearly wet himself. But 'turn the other cheek' jumped into my head and I let him go. The others laughed. I heard a 'fearty' shouted.

Many years later I got a new job. Guess who my boss was – yep, wee Tam. Now he was still wee, but he was very high up in the company and very powerful.

One day he called me into his office.

'You know', he said. 'No-one would ever have admitted it, but they all really admired your guts. It took real courage to do what you did, not the tough guy act that we put on.'

Something on Tam's jacket lapel caught my eye. A small, silver cross.

❶ Why was the writer picked on at school? What names was he called?

❷ Why did he never retaliate?

❸ In what circumstances did he meet 'wee Tam' later in life? What did Tam say to him?

❹ Tam was wearing a small, silver cross. What does this tell you about him?

❺ What is revenge?

❻ What is meant by 'an eye for an eye and a tooth for a tooth?'

❼ 'If anyone slaps you on the right cheek, let him slap your left cheek too.' What do you think this means?

MAKING CONNECTIONS

1 Describe a time when you have witnessed someone being picked on. What were the circumstances? How did the person react? How do you think they felt? What did you do?

2 If a group of pupils started picking on you and making your life miserable, what would you do? Who would you turn to for help?

3 Describe a time when you have wanted to 'get someone back' for something. What were the circumstances? How did you feel about it afterwards?

4 Do you think you could ever find yourself picking on a new person in school? If everyone else started to make fun of the new person, could you join in? Would it be difficult to avoid becoming involved? Why/why not?

5 In groups discuss your ideas for a short story entitled 'Turn the other cheek'. Discuss and prepare a plan for the story then write you own version.

6 Could you forgive someone for picking on you? What would you expect from that person first?

Thinking it over

1 Do you think that the principle of 'an eye for an eye and a tooth for a tooth' is likely to encourage or discourage revenge?

2 Is the principle of 'turning the other cheek' a realistic one for individuals to follow when faced with a conflict situation? What might be the advantages and disadvantages for the people involved?

3 Is the principle of 'turning the other cheek' a realistic one for nations to follow when faced with a potential conflict? Would 'turning the other cheek' provide time for dealing with a situation peacefully or would it be seen as a sign of weakness? Give reasons for your answer.

4 'Turning the other cheek is the bravest thing anyone can do.' Do you agree or disagree?

5
• Retaliation can always be justified.
• Retaliation can sometimes be justified.
• Retaliation can never be justified.

Say which of the above statements you agree with and give reasons to support your view. Conduct a class survey on which of the statements people agreed with. How does the overall class position differ from yours?

4 Making the world a better place: Love for enemies

> You have heard that it was said, 'Love your friends, hate your enemies.' But now I tell you: love your enemies and pray for those who persecute you, so that you may become the sons of your Father in Heaven. (Matthew, 5: 43–5)

Desmond Tutu

For many years, South Africa lived under a system called apartheid where blacks and 'non-whites' experienced discrimination and hardship. Nelson Mandela was imprisoned for many years for opposing the government. Eventually, times changed; Mandela was released, and became the new South Africa's first President. There was no rounding up of those who had done wrong. No revenge attacks by the new government. Instead, Mandela appointed Archbishop Desmond Tutu to set up what became the Truth and Reconciliation Committee. Tutu realised that many wrongs had been committed under apartheid. There wasn't much point in trying to find people to blame. The point was to move on. He brought victims and their persecutors together. He tried to get people to forgive even if they couldn't forget. Perhaps Tutu helped enemies to understand each other, the first step towards loving.

FINDING OUT

❶ What is discrimination? What is apartheid? What discrimination did black people experience under apartheid?

❷ Describe the work of Desmond Tutu in South Africa.

❸ Why do you think the committee was called the Truth and Reconciliation Committee?

❹ What is the difference between reconciliation and forgiveness?

❺ Find out what the flag of South Africa looks like. What are the different meanings attached to it?

❻ Research the life of Desmond Tutu. Find out what he believed and how his beliefs influenced his actions. How could he be said to have put the teachings of Jesus into practice?

MAKING CONNECTIONS

❶ Could the South African example of a Truth and Reconciliation Committee be of use in other situations? What incidents or events among your friends, within your school or in your local community might it be relevant to? How might such a committee be set up? Who would be on it? Who would chair it?

❷ Is it better to make friends or enemies? How can you avoid making enemies? How could you turn a friend into an enemy?

❸ Describe a time when you made up with someone. Was it you that made the first move or the other person? Describe what happened.

Thinking it over

❶ Is it always possible to turn an enemy into a friend? When should you stop trying? What makes it difficult for enemies to be friends? Do you think some people just don't want to be friends? Why do you think this is?

❷ 'Desmond Tutu tried to get people to forgive, even if they couldn't forget.' Even if people can't forget, is it important that they learn to forgive? Why or why not?

❸ Do you think that the approach taken by Mandela and Tutu was the right one? In groups discuss the possible advantages and disadvantages. Do the advantages outweigh the disadvantages or vice versa?

---

stimulus 5

What makes you happy? Money and possessions

In the Sermon on the Mount, Jesus warned against people getting too attached to money and possessions.

> Do not store up riches for yourselves here on earth, where moths and rust destroy, and robbers break in and steal. Instead, store up riches for yourselves in heaven, where moths and rust cannot destroy, and robbers cannot break in and steal. For your heart will always be where your riches are. (Matthew, 6:19–21)

> No one can be a slave of two masters; he will hate one and love the other; he will be loyal to one and despise the other. You cannot serve both God and money. (Matthew, 6:24)

Dave won the lottery! He was as happy as could be. He phoned his boss. 'Hope I never see you again!' he bellowed down the phone. He bought a flashy car, a swanky house, a paradise holiday. He came home. He got new friends. They were always around. Always partying. Everyone wanted to be Dave's

friend. But Dave got tense: 'Don't touch that painting, it's worth thousands!' 'Take off your shoes, it's a Persian rug you know!' 'You can't sit in my car with those trousers!'

A salesman appeared one day selling burglar alarms. Dave bought them all. Then more. Then more. Soon, a different code number was needed for each room in the house.

When Dave's friends arrived a burly security guard quizzed them at the iron gates. Soon this was replaced by a CCTV camera. Then, there were just locked gates. Electric fences. Dave's money sat in the bank and grew. Dave ate richer and richer food, screaming at his chefs to 'get the flavour right!' Dave rarely went out. He was too well known, too easy to kidnap, too easy to ransom.

Dave had everything.

One night a dark figure stood by his safe as Dave tried to remember the combination. 'You must come with me now.' 'No!' screamed Dave, 'I won't be your hostage!' The shadowy figure replied, 'No Dave, there will be no ransom here….' Dave twitched, 'I don't get it, I'm as rich as anyone can be!'

'No Dave… not where you're going,' the dark shape replied.

FINDING OUT

❶ Describe Dave's lifestyle after he won the lottery.

❷ What is meant by 'storing up riches on earth'?

❸ What is meant by 'storing up riches in heaven'?

❹ 'You cannot serve both God and money.' Explain this in your own words.

❺ What could Dave have done to 'store up riches in heaven'?

❻ What happened to Dave?

MAKING CONNECTIONS

❶ Design a poster with the title 'Riches on earth and Riches in heaven'.

❷ What are your most valuable possessions? What is it that gives them value for you?

❸ Do you know anyone who has won a lot of money? Describe the circumstances. Has it changed them in any way – for the better or the worse?

❹ Who wants to be a millionaire? If you won a large amount of money what would you do? What problems might having a lot of money bring?

❺ Money and possessions don't always last – money gets spent and possessions get broken or lost. Are there things you would want to last forever, such as, friendships, happiness, feelings of security? Why?

Thinking it over

❶ What makes some people believe that having a lot of money will solve all their problems?

❷ Do you think that people sometimes get too attached to the things they own? What might be good and bad about that?

❸ Do you think that the richer you are the happier you will be? Why or why not?

❹ 'The love of money is the root of all evil.' What evidence do you think there is to support this view?

❺ Do you think the Lottery is a good thing or a bad thing for those who take part in it? Is there a danger that it encourages people to dream about what life could be like in the future rather than make the most of their life in the present? What do you think?

❻ Did you feel sorry for Dave or do you think he got what he deserved? What do you think went wrong?

stimulus
6 *Don't hide your light*

You are like light for the whole world. A city built on a hill cannot be hidden. No one lights a lamp and puts it under a bowl; instead he puts it on the lamp stand, where it gives light for everyone in the house. In the same way your light must shine before people, so that they will see the good things you do and praise your Father in heaven.
(Matthew, 5:14–16)

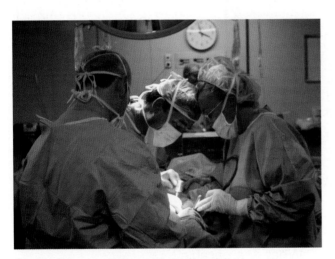

Don't hide your light under a bowl

❶ What happens if you cover a light with a bowl?

❷ Explain in your own words what Jesus is teaching in this passage.

❸ How does the picture illustrate the saying 'Don't hide your light under a bowl'?

MAKING CONNECTIONS

❶ You're sitting in RE and have just read the passage in Stimulus 6. Here are your thoughts, but you'll have to fill in the gaps.

> I know I'm really good at _____ but I don't always let people see this. That's because _____ My RE teacher today said that everyone has a special skill, and that Christians believe that this skill is a gift from God. I think _____
>
> The teacher also said that each of our special skills could make the world a better place. If I put my special skill into practice then _____
>
> Maybe I could start by _____

❷ Create a graffiti wall in your class. Everyone should write on the wall one skill or ability they have which they think they could use to make the world a better place.

stimulus 7 *What is your world based on?*

The Sermon on the Mount ends with a parable. You can read it in Matthew, 7:24–7

❶ In the Sermon on the Mount there is teaching about the following topics:

Adultery	Matthew, 5:27–30
Divorce	Matthew, 5:31–2
Vows	Matthew, 5:33–6
Charity	Matthew, 6:2–4
Judging others	Matthew, 7:1–5

Work in small groups and choose one of the above topics. Write down in your own words what the teaching is and produce a heading to sum up the teaching. Share what you have learnt with the rest of the class.

❷ Look at the parable of the two houses. What is a parable?

❸ Who was the wiser of the two men? Why?

❹ Discuss in class what the parable means and write a paragraph explaining it.

❺ Why do you think this parable is at the end of the Sermon on the Mount?

MAKING CONNECTIONS

❶ Would you say that your life was 'based' on anything? If yes what is it based on?

❷ Create a collage of things in life which you would describe as 'life's storms and floods'.

Thinking it over

❶ Is it important to have values on which your life is based? Why or why not. What values do you think are the most important?

❷ Look at the following statements about Jesus' teachings in the Sermon on the Mount:

- They are too difficult to put into practice.
- They were OK for Jesus' time but not for today's world.
- If everybody tried to follow them the world be a better place.
- They provide a good basis for living your life.

For each, explain why a person might argue that point of view. Which comes nearest your own thinking? Why?

Index